BACK RIDGE

Work only in loops indicated by arrow (*Fig. 1*).

Fig. 1

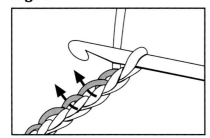

BACK LOOP ONLY

Work only in loop(s) indicated by arrow (*Fig. 2*).

Fig. 2

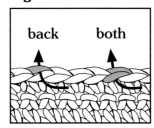

CHANGING COLORS

Work the last stitch to within one step of completion, hook new yarn (*Fig. 3a or 3b*) and draw through all oops on hook. Cut old yarn and work over both ends unless otherwise specified.

Fig. 3a

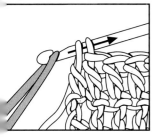

Fig. 3b

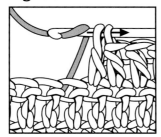

POST STI1

Work around post o
direction of arrow (*I*

Fig. 4

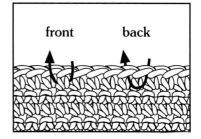

FREE LOOPS OF A CHAIN

When instructed to work in free loops of a chain, work in loop indicated by arrow (*Fig. 5*).

Fig. 5

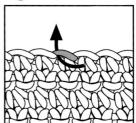

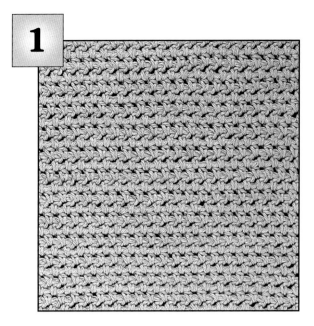

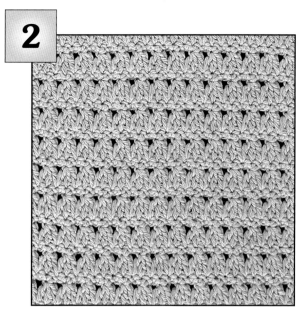

Ch 43.

Row 1 (Right side)**:** Hdc in fifth ch from hook, ★ ch 1, skip next ch, hdc in next ch; repeat from ★ across: 20 sps.

Note: Loop a short piece of yarn around any stitch to mark Row 1 as **right** side.

Row 2: Ch 2 **(counts as first hdc)**, turn; (hdc in next ch-1 sp, ch 1) across to last sp, 2 hdc in last sp: 19 ch-1 sps.

Row 3: Ch 3, turn; (hdc in next ch-1 sp, ch 1) across to last 2 hdc, skip next hdc, hdc in last hdc: 20 sps.

Repeat Rows 2 and 3 until Dishcloth measures approximately 9¹/₂" from beginning ch, ending by working Row 3; do **not** finish off.

Work desired Edging, page 58.

Ch 38.

Row 1 (Wrong side)**:** Sc in second ch from hook and in each ch across: 37 sc.

Note: Loop a short piece of yarn around **back** of any stitch on Row 1 to mark **right** side.

Row 2: Ch 3 **(counts as first hdc plus ch 1)**, turn; (YO, insert hook in **next** sc, YO and pull up a loop, YO and draw through 2 loops on hook) 3 times, YO and draw through all 4 loops on hook, ch 2, ★ YO, insert hook in same sc as last st, YO and pull up a loop, YO and draw through 2 loops on hook, (YO, insert hook in **next** sc, YO and pull up a loop, YO and draw through 2 loops on hook) twice, YO and draw through all 4 loops on hook, ch 2; repeat from ★ across to last sc, hdc in last sc: 19 sts and 18 sps.

Row 3: Ch 1, turn; sc in first hdc and in next 2 chs, (skip next st, sc in next 2 chs) across to last 3 sts, skip next st, sc in next ch and in last hdc: 37 sc.

Repeat Rows 2 and 3 until Dishcloth measures approximately 11" from beginning ch, ending by working Row 3; do **not** finish off.

Work desired Edging, page 58.

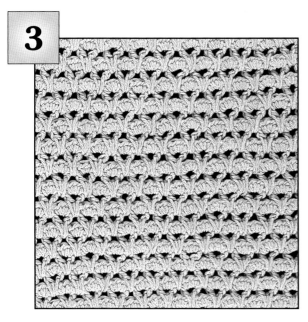

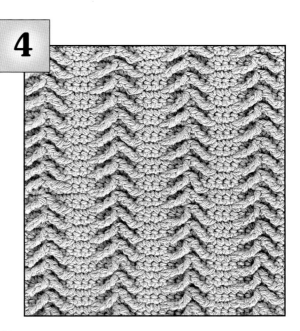

STITCH GUIDE
V-ST
(Dc, ch 3, dc) in st or sp indicated.

Ch 39.

Row 1: Sc in second ch from hook and in each ch across: 38 sc.

Row 2 (Right side)**:** Ch 3 **(counts as first dc, now and throughout)**, turn; skip next sc, work V-St in next sc, (skip next 2 sc, work V-St in next sc) across to last 2 sc, skip next sc, dc in last sc: 12 V-Sts.

Note: Loop a short piece of yarn around any stitch to mark Row 2 as **right** side.

Row 3: Ch 2 **(counts as first hdc, now and throughout)**, turn; 3 hdc in each ch-3 sp across to last 2 dc, skip next dc, hdc in last dc: 38 hdc.

Row 4: Ch 4 **(counts as first dc plus ch 1)**, turn; dc in same st, ★ skip next 3 hdc, working around previous row, work V-St in sp **before** next V-St one row **below** (**between** dc); repeat from ★ across to last 4 hdc, skip next 3 hdc, (dc, ch 1, dc) in last hdc: 11 V-Sts.

Row 5: Ch 2, turn; hdc in first ch-1 sp, 3 hdc in each ch-3 sp across to last ch-1 sp, hdc in last ch-1 sp and in last dc: 37 hdc.

Row 6: Ch 3, turn; skip next hdc, working around previous row, work V-St in sp **before** first V-St one row **below** (**between** dc), ★ skip next 3 hdc, working around previous row, work V-St in sp **before** next V-St one row **below** (**between** dc); repeat from ★ across to last 5 hdc, skip next 3 hdc, working around previous row, work V-St in sp **after** last V-St one row **below** (**between** dc), skip next hdc, dc in last hdc.

Repeat Rows 3-6 until Dishcloth measures approximately 11" from beginning ch, ending by working a **wrong** side row; do **not** finish off.

Work desired Edging, page 58.

Ch 37.

Row 1 (Right side)**:** Sc in second ch from hook and in each ch across: 36 sc.

Note: Loop a short piece of yarn around any stitch to mark Row 1 as **right** side.

Row 2: Ch 1, turn; sc in each st across.

Row 3: Ch 1, turn; sc in first 4 sc, YO 3 times, insert hook from **front** to **back** around post of second sc 2 rows **below** *(Fig. 4, page 2)*, YO and pull up a loop (5 loops on hook), (YO and draw through 2 loops on hook) 3 times, YO 3 times, skip next 5 sts 2 rows **below**, insert hook from **front** to **back** around post of next sc, YO and pull up a loop (6 loops on hook), (YO and draw through 2 loops on hook) 3 times, YO and draw through all 3 loops on hook, skip next sc from last sc made, ★ sc in next 8 sc, YO 3 times, skip next 2 sc 2 rows **below**, insert hook from **front** to **back** around post of next sc, YO and pull up a loop (5 loops on hook), (YO and draw through 2 loops on hook) 3 times, YO 3 times, skip next 5 sts 2 rows **below**, insert hook from **front** to **back** around post of next sc, YO and pull up a loop (6 loops on hook), (YO and draw through 2 loops on hook) 3 times, YO and draw through all 3 loops on hook, skip next sc from last sc made; repeat from ★ 2 times **more**, sc in last 4 sc.

Repeat Rows 2 and 3 until Dishcloth measures approximately 9½" from beginning ch, ending by working Row 2; do **not** finish off.

Work desired Edging, page 58.

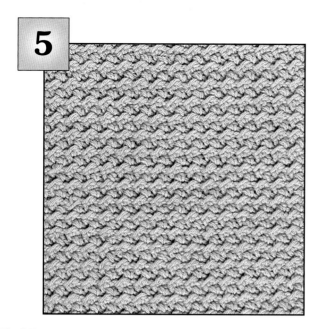

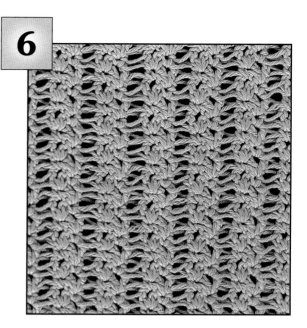

5

Ch 37.

Row 1 (Wrong side)**:** Slip st **loosely** in third ch from hook **(2 skipped chs count as first hdc)**, (hdc in next ch, slip st **loosely** in next ch) across.

Note: Loop a short piece of yarn around **back** of any stitch on Row 1 to mark **right** side.

Row 2: Ch 2 **(counts as first hdc)**, turn; slip st **loosely** in next hdc, (hdc in next slip st, slip st **loosely** in next hdc) across.

Repeat Row 2 until Dishcloth measures approximately 9½" from beginning ch, ending by working a **right** side row; do **not** finish off.

Work desired Edging, page 58.

6

Ch 41.

Row 1 (Right side)**:** Dc in fourth ch from hook **(3 skipped chs count as first dc)**, ★ sc in next ch, pull up loop on hook to measure ¾", skip next 3 chs, (dc, ch 1, dc) in next ch; repeat from ★ across to last 2 chs, skip next ch, sc in next ch: 24 sts and 7 loops.

Note: Loop a short piece of yarn around any stitch to mark Row 1 as **right** side.

Row 2: Ch 3 **(counts as first dc)**, turn; dc in next dc, ★ sc in next ch-1 sp, pull up loop on hook to measure ¾", skip next dc, (dc, ch 1, dc) in next sc; repeat from ★ across to last 2 dc, skip next dc, sc in last dc.

Repeat Row 2 until Dishcloth measures approximately 10" from beginning ch, ending by working a **wrong** side row; do **not** finish off.

Work desired Edging, page 58.

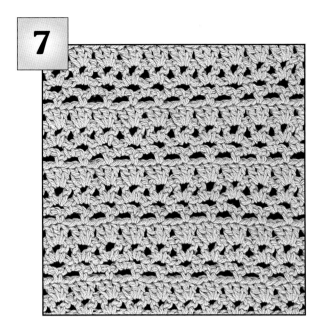

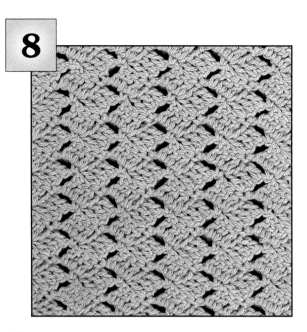

Ch 38.

Row 1 (Wrong side)**:** Dc in fifth ch from hook, ★ skip next 2 chs, (dc, ch 1, dc) in next ch; repeat from ★ across: 12 sps.

Note: Loop a short piece of yarn around **back** of any stitch on Row 1 to mark **right** side.

Row 2: Ch 3 **(counts as first dc)**, turn; 2 dc in first ch-1 sp, 3 dc in each sp across: 36 dc.

Row 3: Ch 1, turn; sc in first 2 dc, ch 3, ★ skip next 2 dc, sc in next dc, ch 3; repeat from ★ across to last 4 dc, skip next 2 dc, sc in last 2 dc: 11 ch-3 sps.

Row 4: Ch 1, turn; sc in first sc, ch 3, (sc in next ch-3 sp, ch 3) across, skip next sc, sc in last sc: 12 ch-3 sps.

Row 5: Ch 4, turn; dc in first ch-3 sp, (dc, ch 1, dc) in each ch-3 sp across: 12 sps.

Repeat Rows 2-5 until Dishcloth measures approximately 10" from beginning ch, ending by working Row 5; do **not** finish off.

Work desired Edging, page 58.

Ch 42.

Row 1 (Wrong side)**:** 2 Dc in third ch from hook, skip next 3 chs, sc in next ch, ★ ch 3, dc in next 3 chs, skip next 3 chs, sc in next ch; repeat from ★ across: 24 sts and 5 ch-3 sps.

Note: Loop a short piece of yarn around **back** of any stitch on Row 1 to mark **right** side.

Row 2: Ch 3, turn; 2 dc in first sc, ★ skip next 3 dc, sc in next ch, ch 3, dc in next 2 chs and in next sc; repeat from ★ across to last 3 sts, skip next 2 dc, sc in next ch.

Repeat Row 2 until Dishcloth measures approximately 9" from beginning ch, ending by working a **wrong** side row; do **not** finish off.

Work desired Edging, page 58.

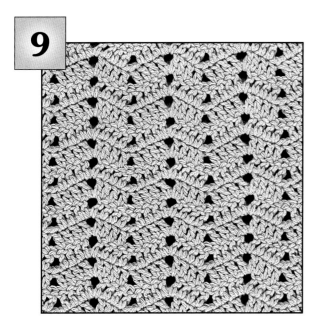

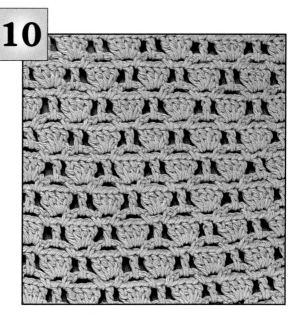

Ch 43.

Row 1 (Wrong side)**:** Dc in fourth ch from hook **(3 skipped chs count as first dc)** and in next 3 chs, ★ skip next 2 chs, dc in next 4 chs, ch 2, dc in next 4 chs; repeat from ★ 2 times **more**, skip next 2 chs, dc in next 3 chs, 2 dc in last ch: 34 dc and 3 ch-2 sps.

Note: Loop a short piece of yarn around **back** of any stitch on Row 1 to mark **right** side.

Row 2: Ch 3 **(counts as first dc)**, turn; dc in same st and in next 3 dc, skip next 2 dc, dc in next 3 dc, ★ (dc, ch 2, dc) in next ch-2 sp, dc in next 3 dc, skip next 2 dc, dc in next 3 dc; repeat from ★ 2 times **more**, 2 dc in last dc.

Repeat Row 2 until Dishcloth measures approximately 10" from beginning ch, ending by working a **wrong** side row; do **not** finish off.

Edging: Ch 1; with **right** side facing, sc evenly around entire Dishcloth working 2 sc in each ch-2 sp and increasing and decreasing as necessary to keep piece lying flat; join with slip st to first sc, finish off.

Ch 46.

Row 1 (Wrong side)**:** Sc in second ch from hook, ★ ch 3, skip next 3 chs, sc in next ch; repeat from ★ across: 11 ch-3 sps.

Note: Loop a short piece of yarn around **back** of any stitch on Row 1 to mark **right** side.

Row 2: Ch 3 **(counts as first dc)**, turn; 4 dc in first ch-3 sp, ★ ch 1, dc in next ch-3 sp, ch 1, 4 dc in next ch-3 sp; repeat from ★ across, dc in last sc: 31 dc and 10 ch-1 sps.

Row 3: Ch 1, turn; sc in first dc, ch 3, (sc in next ch-1 sp, ch 3) across to last 5 dc, skip next 4 dc, sc in last dc: 11 ch-3 sps.

Row 4: Ch 4, turn; dc in first ch-3 sp, ch 1, ★ 4 dc in next ch-3 sp, ch 1, dc in next ch-3 sp, ch 1; repeat from ★ across, dc in last sc: 28 sts and 12 sps.

Row 5: Ch 1, turn; sc in first dc, ch 3, skip first ch-1 sp, (sc in next ch-1 sp, ch 3) across to last dc, skip last dc and next ch, sc in next ch: 11 ch-3 sps.

Repeat Rows 2-5 until Dishcloth measures approximately 9" from beginning ch, ending by working a **wrong** side row; do **not** finish off.

Work desired Edging, page 58.

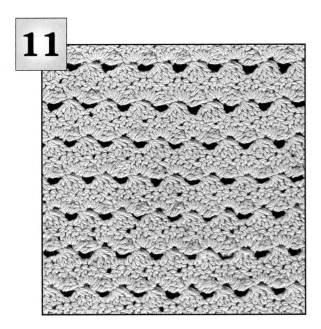

STITCH GUIDE
CLUSTER (uses one ch)
YO, insert hook in third ch from hook, YO and pull up a loop, YO and draw through 2 loops on hook, YO, insert hook in same ch, YO and pull up a loop, YO and draw through 2 loops on hook, YO and draw through all 3 loops on hook.

Ch 40.

Row 1 (Right side): YO, insert hook in fourth ch from hook, YO and pull up a loop, YO and draw through 2 loops on hook, YO, insert hook in next ch, YO and pull up a loop, YO and draw through 2 loops on hook, YO and draw through all 3 loops on hook **(counts as one st)**, ch 3, work Cluster, ★ (YO, insert hook in **next** ch, YO and pull up a loop, YO and draw through 2 loops on hook) 4 times, YO and draw through all 5 loops on hook, ch 3, work Cluster; repeat from ★ across to last 3 chs, (YO, insert hook in **next** ch, YO and pull up a loop, YO and draw through 2 loops on hook) 3 times, YO and draw through all 4 loops on hook: 9 Clusters.

Note: Loop a short piece of yarn around any stitch to mark Row 1 as **right** side.

Row 2: Ch 3 **(counts as first dc, now and throughout)**, turn; 2 dc in same st, (skip next Cluster, 4 dc in next st) across to last Cluster, skip last Cluster, 3 dc in next ch: 38 dc.

Row 3: Ch 6, turn; work Cluster, skip first dc, ★ (YO, insert hook in **next** dc, YO and pull up a loop, YO and draw through 2 loops on hook) 4 times, YO and draw through all 5 loops on hook, ch 3, work Cluster; repeat from ★ across to last dc, dc in last dc: 10 Clusters.

Row 4: Ch 3, turn; (skip next Cluster, 4 dc in next st) across to last Cluster, skip last Cluster, dc in next ch: 38 dc.

Row 5: Ch 3, turn; (YO, insert hook in **next** dc, YO and pull up a loop, YO and draw through 2 loops on hook) twice, YO and draw through all 3 loops on hook, ch 3, work Cluster, ★ (YO, insert hook in **next** dc, YO and pull up a loop, YO and draw through 2 loops on hook) 4 times, YO and draw through all 5 loops on hook, ch 3, work Cluster; repeat from ★ across to last 3 dc, (YO, insert hook in **next** dc, YO and pull up a loop, YO and draw through 2 loops on hook) 3 times, YO and draw through all 4 loops on hook: 9 Clusters.

Repeat Rows 2-5 until Dishcloth measures approximately 10½" from beginning ch, ending by working a **wrong** side row; do **not** finish off.

Work desired Edging, page 58.

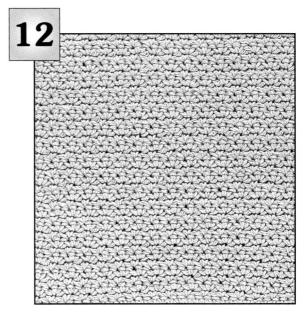

Ch 39.

Row 1 (Wrong side): Sc in second ch from hook and in each ch across: 38 sc.

Note: Loop a short piece of yarn around **back** of any stitch on Row 1 to mark **right** side.

Row 2: Ch 1, turn; skip first sc, 2 sc in next sc, (skip next sc, 2 sc in next sc) across.

Repeat Row 2 until Dishcloth measures approximately 10" from beginning ch, ending by working a **right** side row; do **not** finish off.

Work desired Edging, page 58.

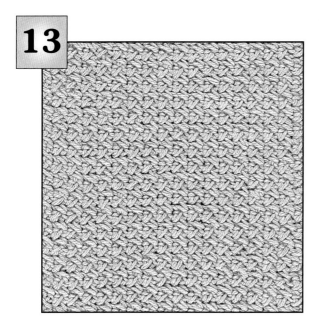

13

Ch 40.

Row 1 (Wrong side)**:** Sc in second ch from hook and in each ch across: 39 sc.

Note: Loop a short piece of yarn around **back** of any stitch on Row 1 to mark **right** side.

Row 2: Ch 1, turn; sc in first sc, ★ skip next sc, sc in next sc, working **loosely** around sc just made, sc in skipped sc; repeat from ★ across.

Repeat Row 2 until Dishcloth measures approximately 9" from beginning ch; do **not** finish off.

Work desired Edging, page 58.

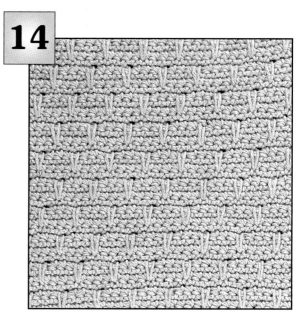

14

STITCH GUIDE
LONG SINGLE CROCHET *(abbreviated LSC)*
Working **around** previous 3 rows, insert hook in sc 3 rows **below** next sc, YO and pull up a loop even with last sc made, YO and draw through both loops on hook.

Ch 36.

Row 1: Sc in second ch from hook and in each ch across: 35 sc.

Row 2 (Right side)**:** Ch 1, turn; sc in each sc across.

Note: Loop a short piece of yarn around any stitch to mark Row 2 as **right** side.

Rows 3-5: Ch 1, turn; sc in each sc across.

Row 6: Ch 1, turn; sc in first 3 sc, (work LSC, sc in next 3 sc) across: 27 sc and 8 LSC.

Rows 7-9: Ch 1, turn; sc in each sc across.

Row 10: Ch 1, turn; sc in first sc, work LSC, (sc in next 3 sc, work LSC) across to last sc, sc in last sc: 26 sc and 9 LSC.

Repeat Rows 3-10 until Dishcloth measures approximately 10" from beginning ch, ending by working a **wrong** side row; do **not** finish off.

Work desired Edging, page 58.

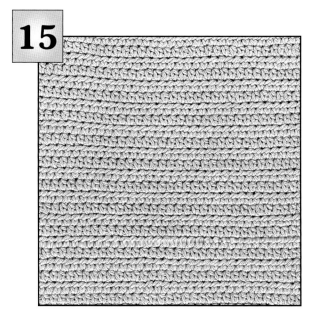

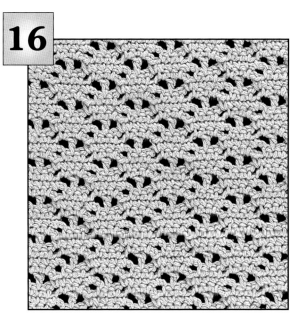

Ch 37.

Row 1 (Right side)**:** Hdc in third ch from hook **(2 skipped chs count as first hdc)** and in each ch across: 36 hdc.

Note: Loop a short piece of yarn around any stitch to mark Row 1 as **right** side.

Row 2: Ch 2 **(counts as first hdc)**, turn; hdc in next hdc and in each hdc across.

Repeat Row 2 until Dishcloth measures approximately 9½" from beginning ch; do **not** finish off.

Work desired Edging, page 58.

Ch 47.

Row 1 (Right side)**:** Sc in second ch from hook and in next 2 chs, ch 2, skip next 2 chs, dc in next ch, ★ ch 2, skip next 2 chs, sc in next 5 chs, ch 2, skip next 2 chs, dc in next ch; repeat from ★ across: 28 sts and 9 ch-2 sps.

Note: Loop a short piece of yarn around any stitch to mark Row 1 as **right** side.

Row 2: Ch 1, turn; sc in first dc and in next ch-2 sp, ch 2, ★ skip next sc, sc in next 3 sc, ch 2, sc in next ch-2 sp, sc in next dc and in next ch-2 sp, ch 2; repeat from ★ across to last 3 sc, skip next sc, sc in last 2 sc.

Row 3: Ch 5 **(counts as first dc plus ch 2)**, turn; sc in next ch-2 sp, ★ sc in next 3 sc and in next ch-2 sp, ch 2, skip next sc, dc in next sc, ch 2, sc in next ch-2 sp; repeat from ★ across to last 2 sc, sc in last 2 sc.

Row 4: Ch 1, turn; sc in first 2 sc, ch 2, sc in next ch-2 sp, ★ sc in next dc and in next ch-2 sp, ch 2, skip next sc, sc in next 3 sc, ch 2, sc in next ch-2 sp; repeat from ★ across to last dc, sc in last dc.

Row 5: Ch 1, turn; sc in first 2 sc and in next ch-2 sp, ch 2, skip next sc, dc in next sc, ★ ch 2, sc in next ch-2 sp, sc in next 3 sc and in next ch-2 sp, ch 2, skip next sc, dc in next sc; repeat from ★ across.

Repeat Rows 2-5 until Dishcloth measures approximately 9½" from beginning ch, ending by working Row 5; do **not** finish off.

Work desired Edging, page 58.

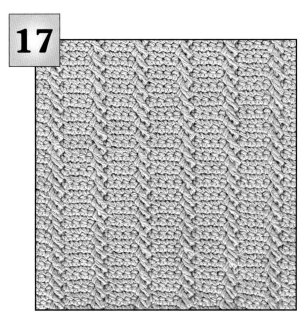

17

STITCH GUIDE
FRONT POST DOUBLE CROCHET
(abbreviated FPdc)
YO, insert hook from **front** to **back** around post of st indicated *(Fig. 4, page 2)*, YO and pull up a loop (3 loops on hook), (YO and draw through 2 loops on hook) twice.

BEGINNING CABLE
Skip next 2 sc, work FPdc around post of next sc, working **behind** FPdc just made, sc in second skipped sc, working in **front** of last FPdc made, work FPdc around post of first skipped sc.

CABLE
Skip next FPdc one row **below** previous row, work FPdc around next FPdc *(Fig. 4, page 2)*, skip sc behind FPdc just made, sc in next sc, working in **front** of last FPdc made, work FPdc around skipped FPdc.

Ch 38.

Row 1: Sc in second ch from hook and in each ch across: 37 sc.

*Note: Work FPdc **loosely** throughout.*

Row 2 (Right side)**:** Ch 1, turn; sc in first 2 sc, work Beginning Cable, ★ skip next sc from last sc made, sc in next 3 sc, work Beginning Cable; repeat from ★ across to last 3 sc, skip next sc from last sc made, sc in last 2 sc: 6 Beginning Cables.

*Note: Loop a short piece of yarn around any stitch to mark Row 2 as **right** side.*

Row 3: Ch 1, turn; sc in each st across: 37 sc.

Row 4: Ch 1, turn; sc in first 2 sc, work Cable, ★ skip next sc from last sc made, sc in next 3 sc, work Cable; repeat from ★ across to last 3 sc, skip next sc from last sc made, sc in last 2 sc.

Repeat Rows 3 and 4 until Dishcloth measures approximately 9½" from beginning ch, ending by working Row 3; do **not** finish off.

Work desired Edging, page 58.

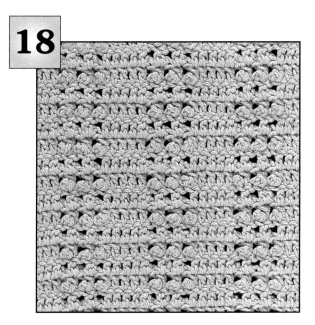

18

STITCH GUIDE
PICOT
Ch 3, slip st in third ch from hook.

Ch 37.

Row 1 (Right side)**:** Dc in fourth ch from hook **(3 skipped chs count as first dc)** and in next 3 chs, ★ work Picot, skip next ch, (dc in next ch, work Picot, skip next ch) twice, dc in next 5 chs; repeat from ★ 2 times **more**: 26 dc.

Note: Loop a short piece of yarn around any stitch to mark Row 1 as **right** side.

Row 2: Ch 3 **(counts as first dc)**, turn; dc in next 4 dc, ★ work Picot, (dc in next dc, work Picot) twice, dc in next 5 dc; repeat from ★ 2 times **more**.

Repeat Row 2 until Dishcloth measures approximately 9" from beginning ch.

Last Row: Ch 3, turn; dc in next 4 dc, ★ ch 1, (dc in next dc, ch 1) twice, dc in next 5 dc; repeat from ★ 2 times **more**; do **not** finish off.

Work desired Edging, page 58.

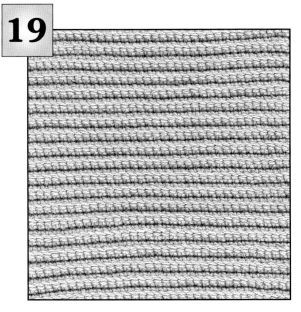

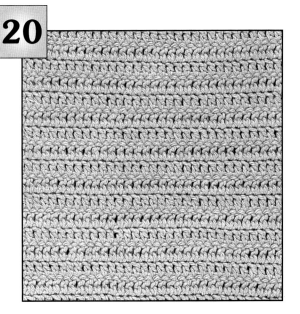

Ch 39.

Row 1 (Right side)**:** Sc in second ch from hook and in each ch across: 38 sc.

Note: Loop a short piece of yarn around any stitch to mark Row 1 as **right** side.

Row 2: Ch 1, turn; sc in Back Loop Only of each sc across *(Fig. 2, page 2)*.

Repeat Row 2 until Dishcloth measures approximately 9" from beginning ch; do **not** finish off.

Work desired Edging, page 58.

Ch 38.

Row 1 (Right side)**:** Dc in fourth ch from hook **(3 skipped chs count as first dc)** and in each ch across: 36 dc.

Note: Loop a short piece of yarn around any stitch to mark Row 1 as **right** side.

Row 2: Ch 3 **(counts as first dc)**, turn; dc in next dc and in each dc across.

Repeat Row 2 until Dishcloth measures approximately 9" from beginning ch; do **not** finish off.

Work desired Edging, page 58.

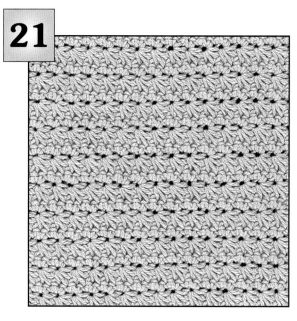

21

Ch 40.

Row 1 (Wrong side)**:** Sc in second ch from hook and in each ch across: 39 sc.

Note: Loop a short piece of yarn around **back** of any stitch on Row 1 to mark **right** side.

Row 2: Ch 3, turn; work Beginning Star St, (ch 1, work Star St) across: 19 Star Sts.

Row 3: Ch 1, turn; 2 sc in eyelet of first Star St, sc in next ch, (sc in eyelet of next Star St and in next ch) across: 39 sc.

Repeat Rows 2 and 3 until Dishcloth measures approximately 9½" from beginning ch, ending by working Row 3; do **not** finish off.

Work desired Edging, page 58.

Design by Darla Sims.

STITCH GUIDE
BEGINNING STAR STITCH
(abbreviated Beginning Star St)
Insert hook in second ch from hook, YO and pull up loop, insert hook in next ch, YO and pull up a loop, insert hook in first sc, YO and pull up a loop, (insert hook in **next** sc, YO and pull up a loop) twice, YO and draw through all 6 loops on hook *(Fig. 6)*. Ch 1 to close Star and form eyelet.

Fig. 6

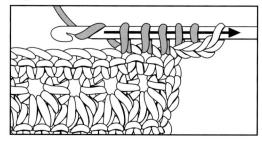

STAR STITCH *(abbreviated Star St)*
Insert hook in eyelet of last Star St (closing ch-1), YO and pull up a loop, insert hook through last 2 loops on left side of last Star St, YO and pull up a loop, insert hook in same sc as last Star St, YO and pull up a loop, (insert hook in **next** sc, YO and pull up a loop) twice, YO and draw through all 6 loops on hook *(Fig. 7)*. Ch 1 to close Star and form eyelet.

Fig. 7

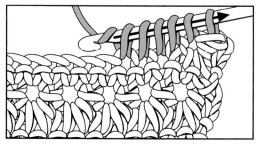

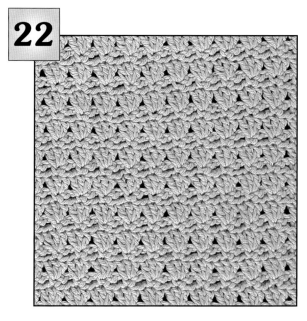

22

Ch 38.

Row 1 (Wrong side)**:** Sc in second ch from hook, ★ ch 2, skip next 2 chs, sc in next ch; repeat from ★ across: 13 sc.

Note: Loop a short piece of yarn around **back** of any stitch on Row 1 to mark **right** side.

Row 2: Ch 3 **(counts as first dc)**, turn; dc in same st, 3 dc in next sc and in each sc across to last sc, 2 dc in last sc: 37 dc.

Row 3: Ch 1, turn; sc in first dc, ★ ch 2, skip next 2 dc, sc in next dc; repeat from ★ across: 13 sc.

Repeat Rows 2 and 3 until Dishcloth measures approximately 9" from beginning ch, ending by working Row 3; do **not** finish off.

Work desired Edging, page 58.

Design by Darla Sims.

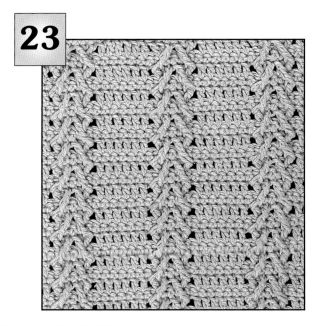

STITCH GUIDE
FRONT POST TREBLE CROCHET
(abbreviated FPtr)

YO twice, insert hook from **front** to **back** around post of st indicated *(Fig. 4, page 2)*, YO and pull up a loop (4 loops on hook), (YO and draw through 2 loops on hook) 3 times.

Ch 40.

Row 1 (Right side)**:** Dc in fourth ch from hook and in next 2 chs, ★ † skip next ch, dc in next 2 chs, working in **front** of last 2 dc made, dc in skipped ch, skip next 2 chs, dc in next ch, working **behind** last dc made, dc in each of 2 skipped chs †, dc in next 6 chs; repeat from ★ once **more**, then repeat from † to † once, dc in last 4 chs: 38 sts.

Note: Loop a short piece of yarn around any stitch to mark Row 1 as **right** side.

Row 2: Ch 1, turn; sc in each st across.

Row 3: Ch 3 **(counts as first dc)**, turn; dc in next 3 sc, ★ † skip next sc, dc in next 2 sc, working in **front** of last 2 dc made, work FPtr around dc one row **below** skipped sc, skip next 2 sc, work FPtr around dc **below** next sc, working **behind** last FPtr made, dc in each of 2 skipped sc †, dc in next 6 sc; repeat from ★ once **more**, then repeat from † to † once, dc in last 4 sc.

Repeat Rows 2 and 3 until Dishcloth measures approximately 10" from beginning ch, ending by working Row 2; do **not** finish off.

Work desired Edging, page 58.

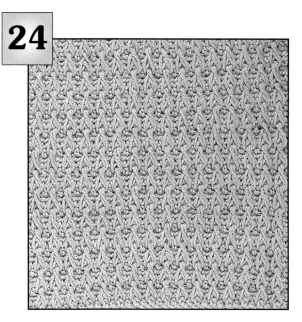

STITCH GUIDE
FRONT POST HALF DOUBLE CROCHET
(abbreviated FPhdc)

YO, insert hook from **front** to **back** around post of st indicated *(Fig. 4, page 2)*, YO and pull up a loop even with loop on hook (3 loops on hook), YO and draw through all 3 loops on hook. Skip hdc behind FPhdc.

Ch 37.

Row 1 (Right side)**:** Hdc in third ch from hook and in each ch across: 35 hdc.

Note: Loop a short piece of yarn around any stitch to mark Row 1 as **right** side.

Row 2: Ch 2, turn; hdc in first hdc and in each st across.

Row 3: Ch 2, turn; hdc in first hdc, (work FPhdc around st one row **below** next hdc, hdc in next hdc) across: 35 sts.

Repeat Rows 2 and 3 until Dishcloth measures approximately 10" from beginning ch, ending by working Row 2; do **not** finish off.

Work desired Edging, page 58.

Design by Darla Sims.

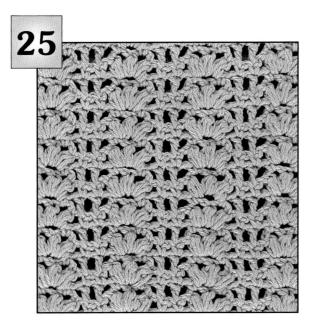

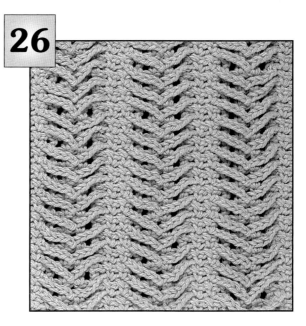

STITCH GUIDE
PUFF ST (uses one ch-3 sp)
★ YO, insert hook in ch-3 sp indicated, YO and pull up a loop; repeat from ★ 2 times **more**, YO and draw through all 7 loops on hook.

Ch 38.

Row 1 (Right side)**:** Sc in second ch from hook and in next ch, ch 1, skip next ch, sc in next ch, ch 3, skip next 2 chs, sc in next ch, ★ (ch 1, skip next ch, sc in next ch) 3 times, ch 3, skip next 2 chs, sc in next ch; repeat from ★ 2 times **more**, ch 1, skip next ch, sc in last 2 chs: 18 sc and 15 sps.

Note: Loop a short piece of yarn around any stitch to mark Row 1 as **right** side.

Row 2: Ch 1, turn; sc in first 2 sc, ch 1, skip next ch-1 sp, work Puff St in next ch-3 sp, (ch 3, work Puff St in same sp) twice, ch 2, skip next ch-1 sp, ★ (sc in next sc, ch 1) twice, skip next ch-1 sp, work Puff St in next ch-3 sp, (ch 3, work Puff St in same sp) twice, ch 2, skip next ch-1 sp; repeat from ★ 2 times **more**, sc in last 2 sc: 22 sts and 19 sps.

Row 3: Ch 3 **(counts as first dc, now and throughout)**, turn; dc in next sc, ch 1, skip next ch-2 sp, sc in next ch-3 sp, ch 3, sc in next ch-3 sp, ch 1, skip next Puff St, ★ (dc in next sc, ch 1) twice, skip next ch-2 sp, sc in next ch-3 sp, ch 3, sc in next ch-3 sp, ch 1, skip next Puff St; repeat from ★ 2 times **more**, dc in last 2 sc: 18 sts and 15 sps.

Row 4: Ch 1, turn; sc in first 2 dc, ch 1, skip next ch-1 sp, work Puff St in next ch-3 sp, (ch 3, work Puff St in same sp) twice, ch 2, skip next ch-1 sp, ★ (sc in next dc, ch 1) twice, skip next ch-1 sp, work Puff St in next ch-3 sp, (ch 3, work Puff St in same sp) twice, ch 2, skip next ch-1 sp; repeat from ★ 2 times **more**, sc in last 2 dc: 22 sts and 19 sps.

Repeat Rows 3 and 4 until Dishcloth measures approximately 9½" from beginning ch, ending by working Row 3; do **not** finish off.

Work desired Edging, page 58.

Ch 40.

Row 1 (Right side)**:** Sc in second ch from hook, ★ ch 1, skip next ch, sc in next ch; repeat from ★ across: 20 sc and 19 ch-1 sps.

Note: Loop a short piece of yarn around any stitch to mark Row 1 as **right** side.

Row 2: Ch 1, turn; sc in first sc, (ch 1, sc in next sc) across.

Row 3: Ch 1, turn; sc in first sc, ch 1, sc in next sc, ★ ch 6, skip next 2 ch-1 sps, working in **front** of previous rows, slip st in skipped ch of beginning ch **below** next ch-1, ch 6, skip next 4 sc on Row 2 from last sc made, sc in next sc, ch 1, sc in next sc; repeat from ★ 2 times **more**.

Row 4: Ch 1, turn; sc in first sc, ch 1, sc in next sc, ★ (ch 1, dc in next sc on Row 2) 4 times, (ch 1, sc in next sc on Row 3) twice; repeat from ★ 2 times **more**.

Row 5: Ch 1, turn; sc in first sc, ch 1, sc in next sc, ★ ch 6, working in **front** of previous row, slip st in skipped ch two rows **above** previous slip st, ch 6, skip next 4 dc on Row 4, sc in next sc, ch 1, sc in next sc; repeat from ★ 2 times **more**.

Row 6: Ch 1, turn; sc in first sc, ch 1, sc in next sc, ★ (ch 1, dc in next dc) 4 times, (ch 1, sc in next sc) twice; repeat from ★ 2 times **more**.

Row 7: Ch 1, turn; sc in first sc, ch 1, sc in next sc, ★ ch 6, working in **front** of previous row, slip st in skipped ch one row **above** previous slip st, ch 6, skip next 4 dc on previous row, sc in next sc, ch 1, sc in next sc; repeat from ★ 2 times **more**.

Repeat Rows 6 and 7 until Dishcloth measures approximately 8½" from beginning ch, ending by working Row 7; do **not** finish off.

Next Row: Ch 1, turn; slip st in first sc, ch 1, slip st in next sc, ★ (ch 1, sc in next dc) 4 times, (ch 1, slip st in next sc) twice; repeat from ★ 2 times **more**.

Last Row: Ch 1, turn; sc in first slip st, ch 1, sc in next slip st, ★ (ch 1, sc in next sc) 4 times, (ch 1, sc in next slip st) twice; repeat from ★ 2 times **more**; do **not** finish off.

Work desired Edging, page 58.

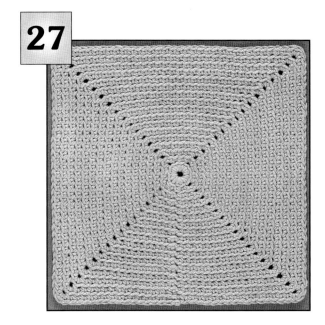

Ch 4; join with slip st to form a ring.

Rnd 1 (Right side)**:** Ch 1, 12 sc in ring; join with slip st to Back Loop Only of first sc *(Fig. 2, page 2)*: 12 sc.

Note #1: Loop a short piece of yarn around any stitch to mark Rnd 1 as **right** side.

Note #2: Work in Back Loops Only throughout.

Rnd 2: Ch 1, sc in same st and in next sc, 3 sc in next sc, (sc in next 2 sc, 3 sc in next sc) around; join with slip st to first sc: 20 sc.

Rnd 3: Ch 1, sc in same st and in next 2 sc, 3 sc in next sc, (sc in next 4 sc, 3 sc in next sc) around to last sc, sc in last sc; join with slip st to first sc: 28 sc.

Rnd 4: Ch 1, sc in same st and in each sc across to center sc of next 3-sc group, 3 sc in center sc, ★ sc in each sc across to center sc of next 3-sc group, 3 sc in next sc; repeat from ★ 2 times **more**, sc in each sc across; join with slip st to first sc.

Repeat Rnd 4 until Dishcloth measures approximately 9¹/₂" square; do **not** finish off.

Work desired Edging, page 58.

Design by Darla Sims.

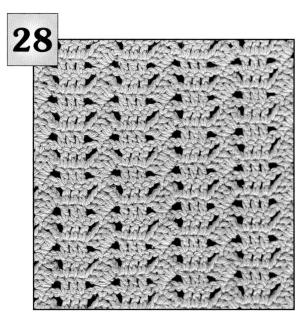

Ch 45.

Row 1 (Right side)**:** Dc in fourth ch from hook **(3 skipped chs count as first dc)** and in next ch, ★ skip next 2 chs, dc in next ch, ch 3, 3 dc around post of last dc made, skip next 2 chs, dc in next 3 chs; repeat from ★ across: 38 dc and 5 ch-3 sps.

Note: Loop a short piece of yarn around any stitch to mark Row 1 as **right** side.

Row 2: Ch 3 **(counts as first dc, now and throughout)**, turn; dc in next 2 dc, ★ ch 2, skip next 3 dc, sc in next ch, ch 2, skip next 2 chs and next dc, dc in next 3 dc; repeat from ★ across: 23 sts and 10 ch-2 sps.

Row 3: Ch 3, turn; dc in next 2 dc, ★ dc in next sc, ch 3, 3 dc around post of last dc made, dc in next 3 dc; repeat from ★ across: 38 dc and 5 ch-3 sps.

Repeat Rows 2 and 3 until Dishcloth measures approximately 10" from beginning ch, ending by working Row 2; do **not** finish off.

Work desired Edging, page 58.

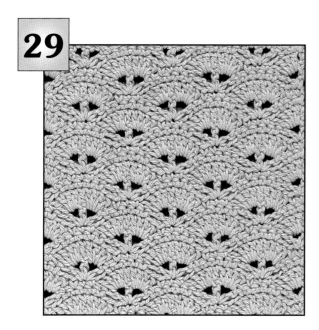

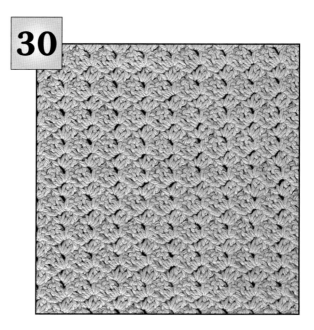

Ch 42.

Row 1 (Wrong side)**:** Dc in sixth ch from hook, skip next 3 chs, sc in next 5 chs, skip next 3 chs, ★ dc in next ch, (ch 2, dc in same ch) twice, skip next 3 chs, sc in next 5 chs, skip next 3 chs; repeat from ★ once **more**, (dc, ch 2, dc) in last ch: 24 sts and 6 sps.

Note: Loop a short piece of yarn around **back** of any stitch on Row 1 to mark **right** side.

Row 2: Ch 3, turn; 4 dc in first ch-2 sp, skip next 2 sts, sc in next 3 sc, 4 dc in next ch-2 sp, ★ dc in next dc, 4 dc in next ch-2 sp, skip next 2 sts, sc in next 3 sc, 4 dc in next sp; repeat from ★ once **more**, dc in third ch of turning ch: 37 sts.

Row 3: Ch 1, turn; sc in first 3 dc, skip next 3 sts, dc in next sc, (ch 2, dc in same sc) twice, skip next 3 sts, ★ sc in next 5 dc, skip next 3 sts, dc in next sc, (ch 2, dc in same sc) twice, skip next 3 sts; repeat from ★ once **more**, sc in next 2 dc and in next ch: 25 sts and 6 ch-2 sps.

Row 4: Ch 1, turn; sc in first 2 sc, 4 dc in next ch-2 sp, dc in next dc, 4 dc in next ch-2 sp, skip next 2 sts, ★ sc in next 3 sc, 4 dc in next ch-2 sp, dc in next dc, 4 dc in next ch-2 sp, skip next 2 sts; repeat from ★ once **more**, sc in last 2 sc: 37 sts.

Row 5: Ch 5, turn; dc in first sc, skip next 3 sts, sc in next 5 dc, skip next 3 sts, ★ dc in next sc, (ch 2, dc in same sc) twice, skip next 3 sts, sc in next 5 dc, skip next 3 sts; repeat from ★ once **more**, (dc, ch 2, dc) in last sc: 24 sts and 6 sps.

Repeat Rows 2-5 until Dishcloth measures approximately 9" from beginning ch, ending by working a **wrong** side row; do **not** finish off.

Work desired Edging, page 58.

Ch 40.

Row 1 (Right side)**:** (Dc, ch 2, sc) in fourth ch from hook **(3 skipped chs count as first dc)**, ★ skip next 2 chs, (2 dc, ch 2, sc) in next ch; repeat from ★ across: 39 sts and 13 ch-2 sps.

Note: Loop a short piece of yarn around any stitch to mark Row 1 as **right** side.

Row 2: Ch 3, turn; (dc, ch 2, sc) in first ch-2 sp, (2 dc, ch 2, sc) in next ch-2 sp and in each ch-2 sp across.

Repeat Row 2 until Dishcloth measures approximately 11" from beginning ch, ending by working a **right** side row; do **not** finish off.

Work desired Edging, page 58.

Design by Darla Sims.

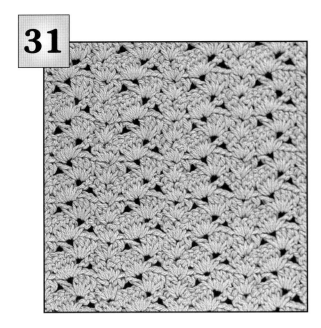

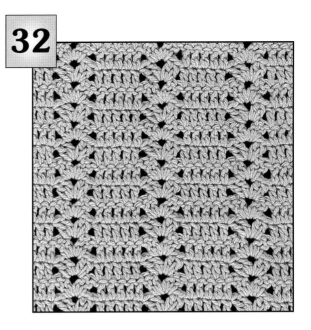

STITCH GUIDE
CLUSTER (uses one st or sp)
★ YO, insert hook in st or sp indicated, YO and pull up a loop, YO and draw through 2 loops on hook; repeat from ★ once **more**, YO and draw through all 3 loops on hook.

Ch 46.

Row 1 (Right side): Work (Cluster, ch 1, Cluster) in seventh ch from hook, ★ skip next 2 chs, (4 dc, ch 1, dc) in next ch, skip next 5 chs, work (Cluster, ch 1, Cluster) in next ch; repeat from ★ across to last 3 chs, ch 1, skip next 2 chs, dc in last ch: 11 sps.

Note: Loop a short piece of yarn around any stitch to mark Row 1 as **right** side.

Row 2: Ch 4, turn; skip first ch-1 sp, work (Cluster, ch 1, Cluster) in next ch-1 sp, ★ (4 dc, ch 1, dc) in next ch-1 sp, work (Cluster, ch 1, Cluster) in next ch-1 sp; repeat from ★ across to last sp, ch 1, skip next ch, dc in next ch.

Repeat Row 2 until Dishcloth measures approximately 10" from beginning ch; do **not** finish off.

Work desired Edging, page 58.

Ch 37.

Row 1 (Right side): Dc in fourth ch from hook **(3 skipped chs count as first dc)** and in next 3 chs, ★ skip next 2 chs, (2 dc, ch 2, 2 dc) in next ch, skip next 2 chs, dc in next 5 chs; repeat from ★ 2 times **more**: 32 dc.

Note: Loop a short piece of yarn around any stitch to mark Row 1 as **right** side.

Row 2: Ch 3 **(counts as first dc)**, turn; dc in next 4 dc, ★ (2 dc, ch 2, 2 dc) in next ch-2 sp, skip next 2 dc, dc in next 5 dc; repeat from ★ 2 times **more**.

Repeat Row 2 until Dishcloth measures approximately 9" from beginning ch; do **not** finish off.

Work desired Edging, page 58.

Design by Darla Sims.

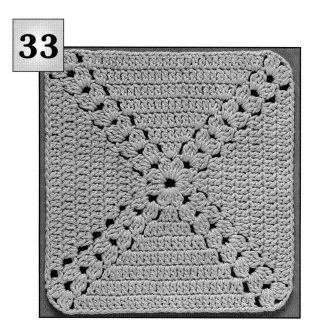

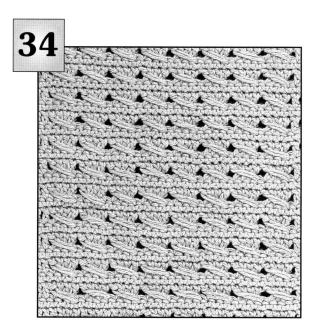

STITCH GUIDE
BEGINNING CLUSTER (uses one sp)
Ch 2, ★ YO, insert hook in sp indicated, YO and pull up a loop, YO and draw through 2 loops on hook; repeat from ★ once **more**, YO and draw through all 3 loops on hook.

CLUSTER (uses one sp)
★ YO, insert hook in sp indicated, YO and pull up a loop, YO and draw through 2 loops on hook; repeat from ★ 2 times **more**, YO and draw through all 4 loops on hook.

Ch 8; join with slip st to form a ring.

Rnd 1 (Right side): Work (Beginning Cluster, ch 5, Cluster) in ring, ch 2, ★ work (Cluster, ch 5, Cluster) in ring, ch 2; repeat from ★ 2 times **more**; join with slip st to top of Beginning Cluster: 8 sps.

Note: Loop a short piece of yarn around any stitch to mark Rnd 1 as **right** side.

Rnd 2: Slip st in first ch-5 sp, work (Beginning Cluster, ch 3, Cluster) in same sp, ch 2, 3 dc in next ch-2 sp, ch 2, ★ work (Cluster, ch 3, Cluster) in next ch-5 sp, ch 2, 3 dc in next ch-2 sp, ch 2; repeat from ★ 2 times **more**; join with slip st to top of Beginning Cluster: 12 dc and 12 sps.

Rnd 3: Slip st in first ch-3 sp, work (Beginning Cluster, ch 3, Cluster) in same sp, ch 2, 2 dc in next ch-2 sp, dc in each dc across to next ch-2 sp, 2 dc in ch-2 sp, ch 2, ★ work (Cluster, ch 3, Cluster) in next ch-3 sp, ch 2, 2 dc in next ch-2 sp, dc in each dc across to next ch-2 sp, 2 dc in ch-2 sp, ch 2; repeat from ★ 2 times **more**; join with slip st to top of Beginning Cluster.

Repeat Rnd 3 until Dishcloth measures approximately 9½" square; do **not** finish off.

Work desired Edging, page 58.

Design by Darla Sims.

Ch 37.

Row 1 (Wrong side): Sc in second ch from hook and in each ch across: 36 sc.

Note: Loop a short piece of yarn around **back** of any stitch on Row 1 to mark **right** side.

Row 2: Ch 3 **(counts as first dc)**, turn; dc in next sc, ★ [skip next sc, dc in next 3 sc, YO, working **loosely** around 3 dc just made, insert hook in skipped sc, YO and pull up a loop even with loop on hook *(Fig. 8)*, (YO and draw through 2 loops on hook) twice **(Slant St made)**]; repeat from ★ across to last 2 sc, dc in last 2 sc.

Fig. 8

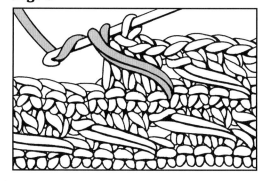

Row 3: Ch 1, turn; sc in each st across.

Repeat Rows 2 and 3 until Dishcloth measures approximately 9½" from beginning ch, ending by working Row 3; do **not** finish off.

Work desired Edging, page 58.

Design by Darla Sims.

19

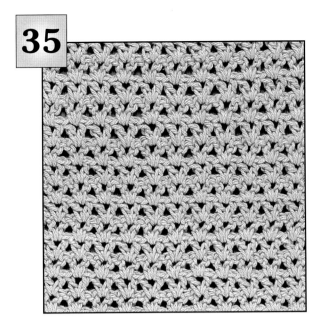

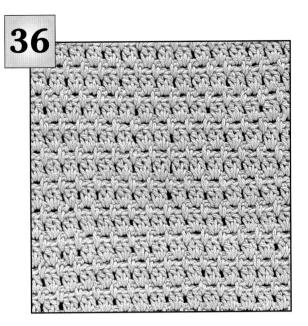

Ch 40.

Row 1 (Wrong side)**:** (Dc, ch 1, dc) in fifth ch from hook, ★ skip next 2 chs, (dc, ch 1, dc) in next ch; repeat from ★ across to last 2 chs, skip next ch, dc in last ch: 12 ch-1 sps.

Note: Loop a short piece of yarn around **back** of any stitch on Row 1 to mark **right** side.

Row 2: Ch 3, turn; (dc, ch 1, dc) in each ch-1 sp across, skip next dc, dc in next ch.

Repeat Row 2 until Dishcloth measures approximately 9" from beginning ch; do **not** finish off.

Work desired Edging, page 58.

Design by Darla Sims.

Ch 36.

Row 1 (Right side)**:** Dc in fourth ch from hook **(3 skipped chs count as first dc)** and in each ch across: 34 dc.

Note: Loop a short piece of yarn around any stitch to mark Row 1 as **right** side.

Row 2: Ch 1, turn; sc in first dc, ch 2, skip next dc, sc in sp **before** next dc, ch 2, ★ skip next 2 dc, sc in sp **before** next dc, ch 2; repeat from ★ across to last 2 dc, skip next dc, sc in last dc: 17 ch-2 sps.

Row 3: Ch 3 **(counts as first dc)**, turn; dc in next ch-2 sp, 2 dc in next ch-2 sp and in each ch-2 sp across to last ch-2 sp, dc in last ch-2 sp and in last sc: 34 dc.

Repeat Rows 2 and 3 until Dishcloth measures approximately 10" from beginning ch, ending by working Row 3; do **not** finish off.

Work desired Edging, page 58.

Design by Darla Sims.

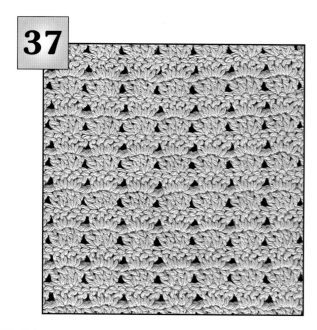

37

Ch 36.

Row 1 (Right side): 2 Dc in fifth ch from hook and in next ch, (skip next 2 chs, 2 dc in each of next 2 chs) across to last 2 chs, skip next ch, dc in last ch: 34 sts.

Note: Loop a short piece of yarn around any stitch to mark Row 1 as **right** side.

Row 2: Ch 3, turn; skip next dc, 2 dc in each of next 2 dc, (skip next 2 dc, 2 dc in each of next 2 dc) across to last dc, skip last dc, dc in next ch.

Repeat Row 2 until Dishcloth measures approximately 9½" from beginning ch; do **not** finish off.

Work desired Edging, page 58.

Design by Darla Sims.

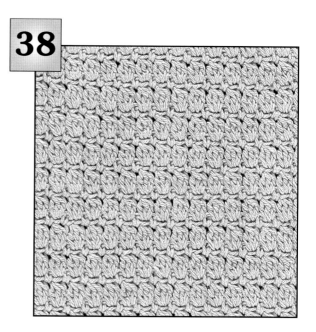

38

STITCH GUIDE
CLUSTER (uses one ch-1 sp)
★ YO, insert hook in ch-1 sp indicated, YO and pull up a loop, YO and draw through 2 loops on hook; repeat from ★ 2 times **more**, YO and draw through all 4 loops on hook.

Ch 38.

Row 1 (Wrong side): Sc in second ch from hook, ★ ch 1, skip next ch, sc in next ch; repeat from ★ across: 19 sc and 18 ch-1 sps.

Note: Loop a short piece of yarn around **back** of any stitch on Row 1 to mark **right** side.

Row 2: Ch 3 **(counts as first dc)**, turn; work Cluster in next ch-1 sp, (ch 1, work Cluster in next ch-1 sp) across to last sc, dc in last sc: 20 sts and 17 ch-1 sps.

Row 3: Ch 1, turn; sc in first dc, ch 1, (sc in next ch-1 sp, ch 1) across to last 2 sts, skip next Cluster, sc in last dc: 19 sc and 18 ch-1 sps.

Repeat Rows 2 and 3 until Dishcloth measures approximately 10" from beginning ch, ending by working Row 3; do **not** finish off.

Work desired Edging, page 58.

Design by Darla Sims.

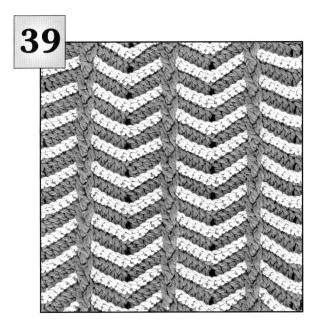

39

STITCH GUIDE
TREBLE CROCHET *(abbreviated tr)*
YO twice, insert hook around st indicated, YO and pull up a loop (4 loops on hook), (YO and draw through 2 loops on hook) 3 times.

With first color, ch 45.

Row 1 (Right side)**:** Working in back ridges of beginning ch *(Fig. 1, page 2)*, dc in fourth ch from hook **(3 skipped chs count as first dc)**, skip next ch, dc in next 5 chs, 3 dc in next ch, dc in next 5 chs, ★ skip next 2 chs, dc in next 5 chs, 3 dc in next ch, dc in next 5 chs; repeat from ★ once **more**, skip next ch, dc in last 2 chs; finish off: 43 dc.

Note: Loop a short piece of yarn around any stitch to mark Row 1 as **right** side.

Row 2: With **wrong** side facing and working in Back Loops Only *(Fig. 2, page 2)*, join next color with slip st in first dc; ch 1, sc in same st and in next dc, skip next dc, sc in next 5 sts, 3 sc in next dc, sc in next 5 sts, ★ skip next 2 dc, sc in next 5 sts, 3 sc in next dc, sc in next 5 sts; repeat from ★ once **more**, skip next dc, sc in last 2 dc; finish off.

Row 3: With **right** side facing and working in Back Loops Only, join next color with slip st in first sc; ch 3 **(counts as first dc)**, dc in next sc, skip next sc, dc in next 5 sc, tr from **front** to **back** around post of center dc of next point one row **below** *(Fig. 4, page 2)*, dc in next sc, tr from **front** to **back** around post of same dc as last tr, dc in next 5 sc, ★ skip next 2 sc, dc in next 5 sc, tr from **front** to **back** around post of center dc of next point one row **below**, dc in next sc, tr from **front** to **back** around post of same dc as last tr, dc in next 5 sc; repeat from ★ once **more**, skip next sc, dc in last 2 sc; finish off.

Rows 4-23: Repeat Rows 2 and 3, 10 times; at end of Row 23, do **not** finish off.

EDGING
FIRST SIDE
Ch 1, sc evenly across end of rows; finish off.

SECOND SIDE
With **right** side facing, join same color as First Side with slip st in end of Row 1; ch 1, sc evenly across end of rows; finish off.

Design by Frances Moore-Kyle.

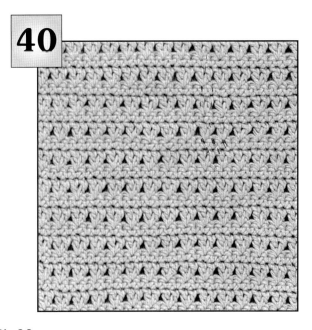

40

Ch 38.

Row 1 (Wrong side)**:** Sc in second ch from hook and in each ch across: 37 sc.

Note: Loop a short piece of yarn around **back** of any stitch on Row 1 to mark **right** side.

Row 2: Ch 3 **(counts as first dc)**, turn; (skip next sc, 2 dc in next sc) across to last 2 sc, skip next sc, dc in last sc: 36 dc.

Row 3: Ch 1, turn; 2 sc in first dc, sc in next dc and in each dc across: 37 sc.

Repeat Rows 2 and 3 until Dishcloth measures approximately 10" from beginning ch, ending by working Row 3; do **not** finish off.

Work desired Edging, page 58.

Design by Darla Sims.

22

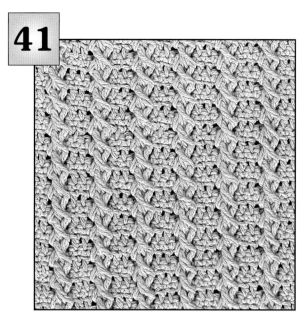

41

STITCH GUIDE
FRONT POST DOUBLE CROCHET
(abbreviated FPdc)
YO, insert hook from **front** to **back** around post of st indicated *(Fig. 4, page 2)*, YO and pull up a loop (3 loops on hook), (YO and draw through 2 loops on hook) twice.

Ch 41.

Row 1 (Right side)**:** Dc in fourth ch from hook **(3 skipped chs count as first dc)** and in each ch across: 39 dc.

Note: Loop a short piece of yarn around any stitch to mark Row 1 as **right** side.

Row 2: Ch 1, turn; sc in each dc across.

Row 3: Ch 3 **(counts as first dc, now and throughout)**, turn; ★ dc in next 2 sc, skip next sc, work FPdc around dc one row **below** next sc, work FPdc around next dc on same row, working in **front** of 2 FPdc just made, work FPdc around dc to **right** of next-to-last FPdc, skip next 3 sc on Row 2 from last dc made; repeat from ★ across to last 3 sc, dc in last 3 sc.

Row 4: Ch 1, turn; sc in each st across.

Row 5: Ch 3, turn; ★ dc in next 2 sc, skip next FPdc one row **below**, work FPdc around each of next 2 FPdc, working in **front** of 2 FPdc just made, work FPdc around skipped FPdc *(Fig. 9)*, skip next 3 sc on previous row from last dc made; repeat from ★ across to last 3 sc, dc in last 3 sc.

Fig. 9

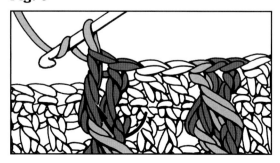

Repeat Rows 4 and 5 until Dishcloth measures approximately 10½" from beginning ch, ending by working Row 4; do **not** finish off.

Work desired Edging, page 58.

Design by Darla Sims.

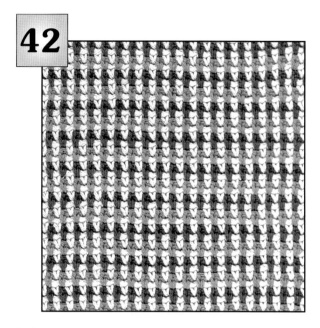

42

With first color, ch 46.

Row 1 (Right side)**:** Sc in second ch from hook, ★ ch 1, skip next ch, sc in next ch; repeat from ★ across; finish off: 23 sc and 22 ch-1 sps.

Note: Loop a short piece of yarn around any stitch to mark Row 1 as **right** side.

Row 2: With **wrong** side facing, join next color with sc in first sc *(see Joining With Sc, page 1)*; sc in next ch-1 sp, (ch 1, sc in next ch-1 sp) across to last sc, sc in last sc; finish off: 24 sc and 21 ch-1 sps.

Row 3: With **right** side facing, join next color with sc in first sc; ch 1, (sc in next ch-1 sp, ch 1) across to last 2 sc, skip next sc, sc in last sc; finish off: 23 sc and 22 ch-1 sps.

Repeat Rows 2 and 3 until Dishcloth measures approximately 9½" from beginning ch, ending by working Row 3; do **not** finish off.

Work desired Edging, page 58.

Design by Terry Kimbrough.

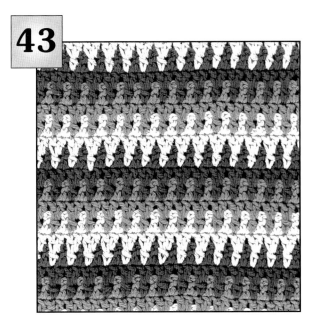

43

STITCH GUIDE
BEGINNING SPLIT TREBLE CROCHET
(abbreviated Beginning Split tr)
YO, insert hook in first ch-1 sp, YO and pull up a loop (3 loops on hook), insert hook in skipped st one row **below** ch-1 *(Fig. 10a)*, YO and pull up a loop (4 loops on hook), insert hook in same ch-1 sp *(Fig. 10b)*, YO and draw though ch-1 sp **and** 2 loops on hook *(Fig. 10c)*, (YO and draw through 2 loops on hook) twice *(Fig. 10d)*.

Fig. 10a

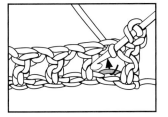

Fig. 10b

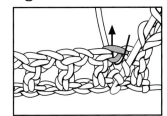

Fig. 10c

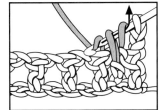

Fig. 10d

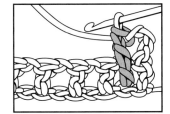

SPLIT TREBLE CROCHET *(abbreviated Split tr)*
YO, insert hook in same ch-1 sp, YO and pull up a loop (3 loops on hook), insert hook in skipped st one row **below** ch-1, YO and pull up a loop (4 loops on hook), insert hook in same ch-1 sp, YO and draw though ch-1 sp **and** 2 loops on hook, (YO and draw through 2 loops on hook) twice.

With first color, ch 40.

Row 1: Place marker in first ch from hook to mark ch-1 sp and in fifth ch from hook to mark skipped st for placement of last Split tr on Row 2, dc in sixth ch from hook, ★ ch 1, skip next ch, dc in next ch; repeat from ★ across changing to next color in last dc *(Fig. 3a, page 2)*: 18 ch-1 sps.

Row 2 (Right side): Ch 3 **(counts as first dc, now and throughout)**, turn; work Beginning Split tr, (dc in next ch-1 sp, work Split tr) across to last 3 chs, dc in next ch leaving last 2 chs unworked: 37 sts.

Note: Loop a short piece of yarn around any stitch to mark Row 2 as **right** side.

Row 3: Ch 4 **(counts as first dc plus ch 1)**, turn; skip next st, dc in next dc, ★ ch 1, skip next st, dc in next dc; repeat from ★ across changing to next color in last dc: 18 ch-1 sps.

Row 4: Ch 3, turn; work Beginning Split tr, (dc in next ch-1 sp, work Split tr) across to last dc, dc in last dc: 37 sts.

Repeat Rows 3 and 4 until Dishcloth measures approximately 10" from beginning ch, ending by working Row 4; do **not** change colors at end of last row and do **not** finish off.

Work desired Edging, page 58.

Design by Ingrid Nielsen.

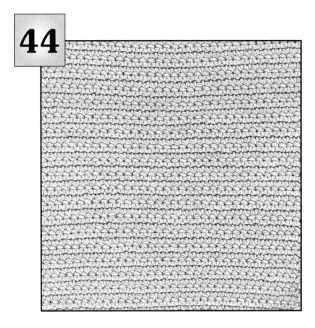

44

Ch 37.

Row 1 (Right side)**:** Sc in second ch from hook and in each ch across: 36 sc.

Note: Loop a short piece of yarn around any stitch to mark Row 1 as **right** side.

Row 2: Ch 1, turn; sc in each sc across.

Repeat Row 2 until Dishcloth measures approximately 9" from beginning ch; do **not** finish off.

Work desired Edging, page 58.

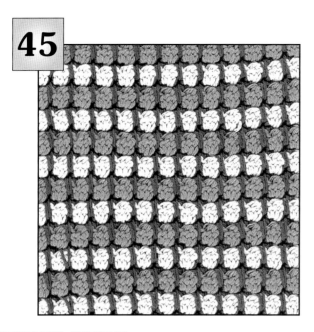

STITCH GUIDE

CLUSTER (uses one sc)
★ YO, insert hook in sc indicated, YO and pull up a loop, YO and draw through 2 loops on hook; repeat from ★ 2 times **more**, YO and draw through all 4 loops on hook.

LONG SINGLE CROCHET *(abbreviated LSC)*
Working **around** next ch, insert hook in skipped sc one row **below**, YO and pull up a loop even with last sc made, YO and draw through both loops on hook.

With first color, ch 38.

Row 1 (Right side)**:** Sc in second ch from hook and in each ch across changing to next color in last sc *(Fig. 3a, page 2)*: 37 sc.

Note: Loop a short piece of yarn around any stitch to mark Row 1 as **right** side.

Row 2: Ch 4 **(counts as first dc plus ch 1)**, turn; ★ skip next st, work Cluster in next sc, ch 1; repeat from ★ across to last 2 sts, skip next st, dc in last sc changing to next color: 17 Clusters.

Row 3: Ch 1, turn; sc in first dc, work LSC, (sc in next Cluster, work LSC) across to last dc, sc in last dc changing to next color: 37 sts.

Repeat Rows 2 and 3 until Dishcloth measures approximately 10" from beginning ch, ending by working Row 3; do **not** change colors at end of last row and do **not** finish off.

Work desired Edging, page 58.

Design by Diana Nelson.

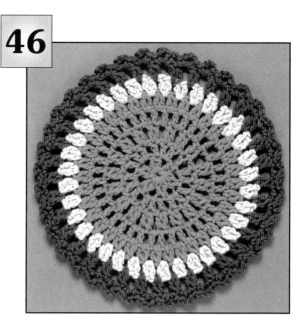

STITCH GUIDE

BEGINNING CLUSTER (uses one st or sp)
Ch 2, YO, insert hook in st or sp indicated, YO and pull up a loop, (YO and draw through 2 loops on hook) twice.

CLUSTER (uses one st or sp)
★ YO, insert hook in st or sp indicated, YO and pull up a loop, YO and draw through 2 loops on hook; repeat from ★ once **more**, YO and draw through all 3 loops on hook.

With first color, ch 4; join with slip st to form a ring.

Rnd 1 (Right side)**:** Work Beginning Cluster in ring, ch 2, (work Cluster in ring, ch 2) 5 times; join with slip st to top of Beginning Cluster: 6 ch-2 sps.

Note: Loop a short piece of yarn around any stitch to mark Rnd 1 as **right** side.

Rnd 2: Ch 4, (dc, ch 1) twice in next ch-2 sp, ★ dc in next Cluster, ch 1, (dc, ch 1) twice in next ch-2 sp; repeat from ★ around; join with slip st to third ch of beginning ch-4: 18 ch-1 sps.

Rnd 3: Work Beginning Cluster in same st, ch 2, (work Cluster in next dc, ch 2) around; join with slip st to top of Beginning Cluster: 18 Clusters.

Rnd 4: Ch 4, dc in next ch-2 sp, ch 1, ★ dc in next Cluster, ch 1, dc in next ch-2 sp, ch 1; repeat from ★ around; join with slip st to third ch of beginning ch-4: 36 ch-1 sps.

Rnd 5: Slip st in first ch-1 sp, work Beginning Cluster in same sp, ch 1, (work Cluster in next ch-1 sp, ch 1) around; join with slip st to top of Beginning Cluster, finish off.

Rnd 6: With **right** side facing, join next color with slip st in any ch-1 sp; ch 4, dc in same sp, ch 1, (dc, ch 1) twice in each ch-1 sp around; join with slip st to third ch of beginning ch-4, finish off: 72 ch-1 sps.

Rnd 7: With **right** side facing, join next color with slip st in last ch-1 sp made; work Beginning Cluster in same sp, ch 2, skip next ch-1 sp, ★ work Cluster in next ch-1 sp, ch 2, skip next ch-1 sp; repeat from ★ around; join with slip st to top of Beginning Cluster: 36 Clusters.

Rnd 8: Slip st in first ch-2 sp, ch 1, (sc, ch 3, sc) in same sp and in each ch-2 sp around; join with slip st to first sc, finish off.

Design by Jennine Korejko.

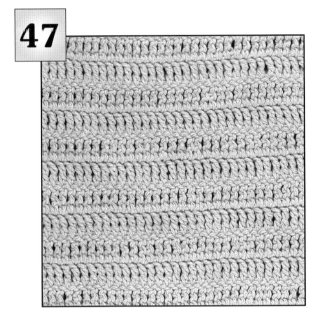

STITCH GUIDE
TREBLE CROCHET *(abbreviated tr)*
YO twice, insert hook in st indicated, YO and pull up a loop (4 loops on hook), (YO and draw through 2 loops on hook) 3 times.

Ch 39.

Row 1 (Right side)**:** Tr in fifth ch from hook **(4 skipped chs count as first tr)** and in each ch across: 36 tr.

Note: Loop a short piece of yarn around any stitch to mark Row 1 as **right** side.

Row 2: Ch 4 **(counts as first tr)**, turn; tr in next tr and in each tr across.

Repeat Row 2 until Dishcloth measures approximately 9" from beginning ch; do **not** finish off.

Work desired Edging, page 58.

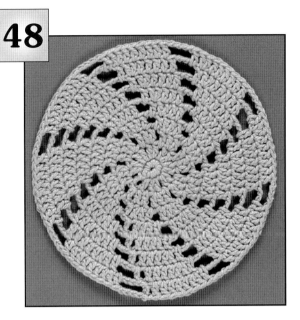

Ch 4; join with slip st to form a ring.

Rnd 1 (Right side)**:** Ch 1, 8 sc in ring; join with slip st to first sc.

Rnd 2: Ch 3 **(counts as first dc, now and throughout)**, dc in same st, ch 1, (2 dc in next sc, ch 1) around; join with slip st to first dc: 16 dc.

Rnd 3: Slip st in next dc, ch 3, dc in same st and in next ch-1 sp, ch 2, skip next dc, ★ 2 dc in next dc, dc in next ch-1 sp, ch 2, skip next st; repeat from ★ around; join with slip st to first dc: 24 dc.

Rnd 4: Slip st in next dc, ch 3, 2 dc in next dc, dc in next ch-2 sp, ch 2, skip next dc, ★ dc in next dc, 2 dc in next dc, dc in next ch-2 sp, ch 2, skip next st; repeat from ★ around; join with slip st to first dc: 32 dc.

Rnd 5: Slip st in next dc, ch 3, dc in next dc, 2 dc in next dc, dc in next ch-2 sp, ch 3, skip next dc, ★ dc in next 2 dc, 2 dc in next dc, dc in next ch-2 sp, ch 3, skip next st; repeat from ★ around; join with slip st to first dc: 40 dc.

Rnds 6 and 7: Slip st in next dc, ch 3, ★ dc in next dc and in each dc across to within one dc of next ch-3 sp, 2 dc in next dc, dc in next ch-3 sp, ch 3, skip next st; repeat from ★ around; join with slip st to first dc: 56 dc.

Rnds 8 and 9: Slip st in next dc, ch 3, ★ dc in next dc and in each dc across to within one dc of next sp, 2 dc in next dc, dc in next sp, ch 4, skip next st; repeat from ★ around; join with slip st to first dc.

Finish off.

Design by Sarah J. Green.

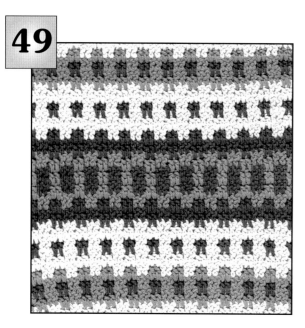

49

With first color, ch 49.

Row 1: Sc in second ch from hook, ch 2, ★ skip next 2 chs, sc in next 2 chs, ch 2; repeat from ★ across to last 3 chs, skip next 2 chs, sc in last ch: 24 sc and 12 ch-2 sps.

Row 2 (Right side)**:** Ch 1, turn; sc in first sc, working in **front** of next ch-2, dc in 2 skipped chs one row **below**, ★ ch 2, skip next 2 sc, working in **front** of next ch-2, dc in 2 skipped chs one row **below**; repeat from ★ across to last sc, sc in last sc: 26 sts and 11 ch-2 sps.

Note: Loop a short piece of yarn around any stitch to mark Row 2 as **right** side.

Row 3: Ch 1, turn; sc in first sc, ch 2, ★ skip next 2 dc, working **behind** next ch-2, dc in 2 skipped sc one row **below**, ch 2; repeat from ★ across to last 3 sts, skip next 2 dc, sc in last sc; finish off: 24 sts and 12 ch-2 sps.

Row 4: With **right** side facing, join next color with sc in first sc *(see Joining With Sc, page 1)*; working in **front** of next ch-2, dc in 2 skipped dc one row **below**, ★ ch 2, skip next 2 dc, working in **front** of next ch-2, dc in 2 skipped dc one row **below**; repeat from ★ across to last sc, sc in last sc: 26 sts and 11 ch-2 sps.

Row 5: Ch 1, turn; sc in first sc, ch 2, ★ skip next 2 dc, working **behind** next ch-2, dc in 2 skipped dc one row **below**, ch 2; repeat from ★ across to last 3 sts, skip next 2 dc, sc in last sc; finish off: 24 sts and 12 ch-2 sps.

Row 6: With **right** side facing, join next color with sc in first sc; working in **front** of next ch-2, dc in 2 skipped dc one row **below**, ★ ch 2, skip next 2 dc, working in **front** of next ch-2, dc in 2 skipped dc one row **below**; repeat from ★ across to last sc, sc in last sc; finish off: 26 sts and 11 ch-2 sps.

Row 7: With **wrong** side facing, join next color with sc in first sc; ch 2, ★ skip next 2 dc, working **behind** next ch-2, dc in 2 skipped dc one row **below**, ch 2; repeat from ★ across to last 3 sts, skip next 2 dc, sc in last sc: 24 sts and 12 ch-2 sps.

Row 8: Ch 1, turn; sc in first sc, working in **front** of next ch-2, dc in 2 skipped dc one row **below**, ★ ch 2, skip next 2 dc, working in **front** of next ch-2, dc in 2 skipped dc one row **below**; repeat from ★ across to last sc, sc in last sc; finish off: 26 sts and 11 ch-2 sps.

Row 9: With **wrong** side facing, join next color with sc in first sc; ch 2, ★ skip next 2 dc, working **behind** next ch-2, dc in 2 skipped dc one row **below**, ch 2; repeat from ★ across to last 3 sts, skip next 2 dc, sc in last sc: 24 sts and 12 ch-2 sps.

Row 10: Ch 1, turn; sc in first sc, working in **front** of next ch-2, dc in 2 skipped dc one row **below**, ★ ch 2, skip next 2 dc, working in **front** of next ch-2, dc in 2 skipped dc one row **below**; repeat from ★ across to last sc, sc in last sc: 26 sts and 11 ch-2 sps.

Row 11: Ch 1, turn; sc in first sc, ch 2, ★ skip next 2 dc, working **behind** next ch-2, dc in 2 skipped dc one row **below**, ch 2; repeat from ★ across to last 3 sts, skip next 2 dc, sc in last sc; finish off: 24 sts and 12 ch-2 sps.

Row 12: With **right** side facing, join next color with sc in first sc; working in **front** of next ch-2, dc in 2 skipped dc one row **below**, ★ ch 2, skip next 2 dc, working in **front** of next ch-2, dc in 2 skipped dc one row **below**; repeat from ★ across to last sc, sc in last sc; finish off: 26 sts and 11 ch-2 sps.

Rows 13-15: Repeat Rows 9-11: 24 sts and 12 ch-2 sps.

Row 16: With **right** side facing, join next color with sc in first sc; working in **front** of next ch-2, dc in 2 skipped dc one row **below**, ★ ch 2, skip next 2 dc, working in **front** of next ch-2, dc in 2 skipped dc one row **below**; repeat from ★ across to last sc, sc in last sc: 26 sts and 11 ch-2 sps.

Row 17: Ch 1, turn; sc in first sc, ch 2, ★ skip next 2 dc, working **behind** next ch-2, dc in 2 skipped dc one row **below**, ch 2; repeat from ★ across to last 3 sts, skip next 2 dc, sc in last sc: 24 sts and 12 ch-2 sps.

Rows 18-20: Repeat Rows 8 and 9 once, then repeat Row 8 once **more**: 26 sts and 11 ch-2 sps.

Row 21: With **wrong** side facing, join next color with sc in first sc; ch 2, ★ skip next 2 dc, working **behind** next ch-2, dc in 2 skipped dc one row **below**, ch 2; repeat from ★ across to last 3 sts, skip next 2 dc, sc in last sc; finish off: 24 sts and 12 ch-2 sps.

Row 22: With **right** side facing, join next color with sc in first sc; working in **front** of next ch-2, dc in 2 skipped dc one row **below**, ★ ch 2, skip next 2 dc, working in **front** of next ch-2, dc in 2 skipped dc one row **below**; repeat from ★ across to last sc, sc in last sc; finish off: 26 sts and 11 ch-2 sps.

Row 23: With **wrong** side facing, join next color with sc in first sc; ch 2, ★ skip next 2 dc, working **behind** next ch-2, dc in 2 skipped dc one row **below**, ch 2; repeat from ★ across to last 3 sts, skip next 2 dc, sc in last sc; finish off: 24 sts and 12 ch-2 sps.

Row 24: With **right** side facing, join next color with sc in first sc; working in **front** of next ch-2, dc in 2 skipped dc one row **below**, ★ ch 2, skip next 2 dc, working in **front** of next ch-2, dc in 2 skipped dc one row **below**; repeat from ★ across to last sc, sc in last sc: 26 sts and 11 ch-2 sps.

Row 25: Ch 1, turn; sc in first sc, ch 2, ★ skip next 2 dc, working **behind** next ch-2, dc in 2 skipped dc one row **below**, ch 2; repeat from ★ across to last 3 sts, skip next 2 dc, sc in last sc; finish off: 24 sts and 12 ch-2 sps.

Rows 26-28: Repeat Rows 16-18: 26 sts and 11 ch-2 sps.

Rows 29-35: Repeat Rows 9-12 once, then repeat Rows 9-11 once **more**: 24 sts and 12 ch-4 sps.

Rows 36-41: Repeat Rows 4-9.

Row 42: Ch 1, turn; sc in first sc, working in **front** of next ch-2, dc in 2 skipped dc one row **below**, ★ sc in next 2 dc, working in **front** of next ch-2, dc in 2 skipped dc one row **below**; repeat from ★ across to last sc, sc in last sc; do **not** finish off.

Work desired Edging, page 58.

Design by Anne Halliday.

With first color, ch 48.

Row 1 (Right side)**:** Sc in second ch from hook and in next 4 chs, 3 sc in next ch, ★ sc in next 3 chs, skip next 2 chs, sc in next 3 chs, 3 sc in next ch; repeat from ★ across to last 5 chs, sc in last 5 chs changing to next color in last sc *(Fig. 3a, page 2)*: 49 sc.

Note #1: Loop a short piece of yarn around any stitch to mark Row 1 as **right** side.

Note #2: Work in Back Loops Only throughout *(Fig. 2, page 2)*.

Rows 2-4: Ch 1, turn; pull up a loop in first 2 sts, YO and draw through all 3 loops on hook, sc in next 4 sc, 3 sc in next sc, ★ sc in next 3 sc, skip next 2 sc, sc in next 3 sc, 3 sc in next sc; repeat from ★ across to last 6 sts, sc in next 4 sc, pull up a loop in last 2 sts, YO and draw through all 3 loops on hook.

Finish off.

Row 5: With **right** side facing, join next color with slip st in first st; ch 1, pull up a loop in same st and in next sc, YO and draw through all 3 loops on hook, sc in next 4 sc, 3 sc in next sc, ★ sc in next 3 sc, skip next 2 sc, sc in next 3 sc, 3 sc in next sc; repeat from ★ across to last 6 sts, sc in next 4 sc, pull up a loop in last 2 sts, YO with next color and draw through all 3 loops on hook.

Repeat Rows 2-5 until Dishcloth measures approximately 9½" from beginning ch, ending by working Row 5; do **not** change colors at end of last row and do **not** finish off.

Edging: Ch 1, do **not** turn; sc evenly around entire Dishcloth increasing and decreasing as necessary to keep piece lying flat; join with slip st to first sc, finish off.

Design by Carole Prior.

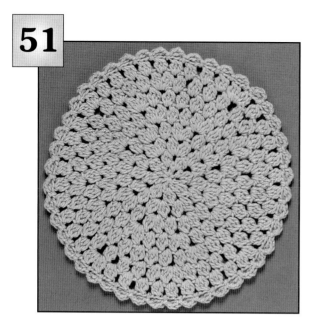

51

STITCH GUIDE

BEGINNING CLUSTER (uses one sp)
Ch 2, ★ YO, insert hook in sp indicated, YO and pull up a loop, YO and draw through 2 loops on hook; repeat from ★ once **more**, YO and draw through all 3 loops on hook.

CLUSTER (uses one sp)
★ YO, insert hook in sp indicated, YO and pull up a loop, YO and draw through 2 loops on hook; repeat from ★ 2 times **more**, YO and draw through all 4 loops on hook.

Rnd 1 (Right side)**:** Ch 5, dc in fifth ch from hook, ch 1, (dc in same ch, ch 1) 6 times; join with slip st to fourth ch of beginning ch-5: 8 ch-1 sps.

Rnd 2: Slip st in first ch-1 sp, work Beginning Cluster in same sp, ch 2, (work Cluster in next ch-1 sp, ch 2) around; join with slip st to top of Beginning Cluster.

Rnd 3: Slip st in first ch-2 sp, work (Beginning Cluster, ch 2, Cluster) in same sp, ch 2, (work Cluster, ch 2) twice in each ch-2 sp around; join with slip st to top of Beginning Cluster: 16 ch-2 sps.

Rnd 4: Slip st in first ch-2 sp, work (Beginning Cluster, ch 2, Cluster) in same sp, ch 2, work Cluster in next ch-2 sp, ch 2, ★ (work Cluster, ch 2) twice in next ch-2 sp, work Cluster in next ch-2 sp, ch 2; repeat from ★ around; join with slip st to top of Beginning Cluster: 24 ch-2 sps.

Rnd 5: Slip st in first ch-2 sp, work Beginning Cluster in same sp, ch 2, work Cluster in next ch-2 sp, ch 2, (work Cluster, ch 2) twice in next ch-2 sp, ★ (work Cluster in next ch-2 sp, ch 2) twice, (work Cluster, ch 2) twice in next ch-2 sp; repeat from ★ around; join with slip st to top of Beginning Cluster: 32 ch-2 sps.

Rnd 6: Slip st in first ch-2 sp, work Beginning Cluster in same sp, ch 2, (work Cluster in next ch-2 sp, ch 2) 6 times, (work Cluster, ch 2) twice in next ch-2 sp, ★ (work Cluster in next ch-2 sp, ch 2) 7 times, (work Cluster, ch 2) twice in next ch-2 sp; repeat from ★ 2 times **more**; join with slip st to top of Beginning Cluster: 36 ch-2 sps.

Rnd 7: Slip st in first ch-2 sp, work Beginning Cluster in same sp, ch 2, (work Cluster in next ch-2 sp, ch 2) 4 times, (work Cluster, ch 2) twice in next ch-2 sp, ★ (work Cluster in next ch-2 sp, ch 2) 8 times, (work Cluster, ch 2) twice in next ch-2 sp; repeat from ★ 2 times **more**, (work Cluster in next ch-2 sp, ch 2) 3 times; join with slip st to top of Beginning Cluster: 40 ch-2 sps.

Rnd 8: Slip st in first ch-2 sp, work (Beginning Cluster, ch 2, Cluster) in same sp, ch 2, (work Cluster in next ch-2 sp, ch 2) 9 times, ★ (work Cluster, ch 2) twice in next ch-2 sp, (work Cluster in next ch-2 sp, ch 2) 9 times; repeat from ★ 2 times **more**; join with slip st to top of Beginning Cluster: 44 ch-2 sps.

Rnd 9: ★ Slip st in next ch-2 sp, ch 3, dc in third ch from hook; repeat from ★ around; join with slip st to first slip st, finish off.

Design by Lois Phillips.

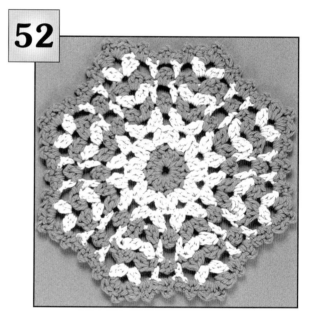

52

STITCH GUIDE

BEGINNING CLUSTER (use one st or sp)
Ch 2, YO, insert hook in st or sp indicated, YO and pull up a loop, (YO and draw through 2 loops on hook) twice.

CLUSTER (use one st or sp)
★ YO, insert hook in st or sp indicated, YO and pull up a loop, YO and draw through 2 loops on hook; repeat from ★ once **more**, YO and draw through all 3 loops on hook.

With first color, ch 5; join with slip st to form a ring.

Rnd 1 (Right side)**:** Ch 3, 15 dc in ring; join with slip st to top of beginning ch-3, finish off: 16 sts.

Note: Loop a short piece of yarn around any stitch to mark Rnd 1 as **right** side.

Rnd 2: With **right** side facing, join next color with slip st in same st as joining; work (Beginning Cluster, ch 3, Cluster) in same st, skip next dc, ★ work (Cluster, ch 3, Cluster) in next dc, skip next dc; repeat from ★ around; join with slip st to top of Beginning Cluster: 8 ch-3 sps.

Rnd 3: Slip st in first ch-3 sp, work (Beginning Cluster, ch 3, Cluster) in same sp, ch 1, ★ work (Cluster, ch 3, Cluster) in next ch-3 sp, ch 1; repeat from ★ around; join with slip st to top of Beginning Cluster, finish off: 16 sps.

Rnd 4: With **right** side facing, join next color with slip st in any ch-3 sp; work (Beginning Cluster, ch 3, Cluster) in same sp, ch 1, (sc, ch 3, slip st) in next ch-1 sp, ch 1, ★ work (Cluster, ch 3, Cluster) in next ch-3 sp, ch 1, (sc, ch 3, slip st) in next ch-1 sp, ch 1; repeat from ★ around; join with slip st to top of Beginning Cluster, finish off: 32 sps.

Rnd 5: With **right** side facing, join next color with slip st in first ch-3 sp; work (Beginning Cluster, ch 3, Cluster) in same sp, dc in next ch-1 sp, ch 2, skip next ch-3 sp, dc in next ch-1 sp, ★ work (Cluster, ch 3, Cluster) in next ch-3 sp, dc in next ch-1 sp, ch 2, skip next ch-3 sp, dc in next ch-1 sp; repeat from ★ around; join with slip st to top of Beginning Cluster, finish off: 16 sps.

Rnd 6: With **right** side facing, join next color with slip st in any ch-3 sp; work (Beginning Cluster, ch 3, Cluster) in same sp, sc in next dc, ch 1, (sc, ch 3, slip st) in next ch-2 sp, ch 1, sc in next dc, ★ work (Cluster, ch 3, Cluster) in next ch-3 sp, sc in next dc, ch 1, (sc, ch 3, slip st) in next ch-2 sp, ch 1, sc in next dc; repeat from ★ around; join with slip st to top of Beginning Cluster, finish off: 32 sps.

Rnd 7: With **right** side facing, join next color with slip st in first ch-3 sp; work (Beginning Cluster, ch 3, Cluster) in same sp, ch 1, dc in next ch-1 sp, ch 2, skip next ch-3 sp, dc in next ch-1 sp, ch 1, ★ work (Cluster, ch 3, Cluster) in next ch-3 sp, ch 1, dc in next ch-1 sp, ch 2, skip next ch-3 sp, dc in next ch-1 sp, ch 1; repeat from ★ around; join with slip st to top of Beginning Cluster, finish off.

Rnd 8: With **right** side facing, join next color with slip st in any ch-3 sp; work (Beginning Cluster, ch 1, sc, ch 3, slip st, ch 1, Cluster) in same sp, ch 1, (sc, ch 3, slip st) in next ch-1 sp, ch 1, [sc in next dc, ch 1, (sc, ch 3, slip st) in next sp, ch 1] twice, ★ work (Cluster, ch 1, sc, ch 3, slip st, ch 1, Cluster) in next ch-3 sp, ch 1, (sc, ch 3, slip st) in next ch-1 sp, ch 1, [sc in next dc, ch 1, (sc, ch 3, slip st) in next sp, ch 1] twice; repeat from ★ around; join with slip st to top of Beginning Cluster, finish off.

Design by Katherine Satterfield.

53

Ch 4; join with slip st to form a ring.

Rnd 1 (Right side)**:** Ch 5, (dc in ring, ch 2) 5 times; join with slip st to third ch of beginning ch-5: 6 ch-2 sps.

Rnd 2: Ch 3, 4 dc in next ch-2 sp, (dc in next dc, 4 dc in next ch-2 sp) around; join with slip st to top of beginning ch-3: 30 sts.

Rnd 3: Ch 4, (dc in next dc, ch 1) around; join with slip st to third ch of beginning ch-4: 30 ch-1 sps.

Rnd 4: Ch 3, dc in each ch-1 sp and in each dc around; join with slip st to top of beginning ch-3: 60 sts.

Rnd 5: Ch 5, skip next dc, ★ dc in next dc, ch 2, skip next dc; repeat from ★ around; join with slip st to third ch of beginning ch-5: 30 ch-2 sps.

Rnd 6: Ch 3, 2 dc in next ch-2 sp, (dc in next dc, 2 dc in next ch-2 sp) around; join with slip st to top of beginning ch-3: 90 sts.

Rnd 7: Ch 1, sc in same st, ★ ch 5, skip next 2 dc, sc in next dc; repeat from ★ around to last 2 dc, ch 2, skip last 2 dc, dc in first sc to form last ch-5 sp: 30 ch-5 sps.

Rnd 8: Ch 1, sc in same sp, (ch 5, sc in next ch-5 sp) around, ch 2, dc in first sc to form last ch-5 sp.

Rnd 9: Ch 1, sc in same sp, (5 dc, ch 3, slip st in top of last dc made, 4 dc) in next ch-5 sp, ★ sc in next ch-5 sp, (5 dc, ch 3, slip st in top of last dc made, 4 dc) in next ch-5 sp; repeat from ★ around; join with slip st to first sc, finish off.

Design by Lois Phillips.

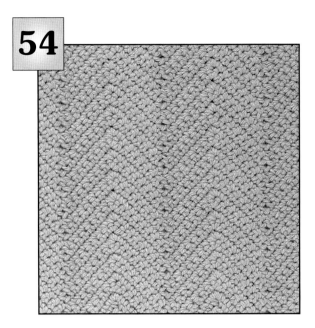

54

Ch 50.

Row 1 (Right side)**:** 2 Sc in second ch from hook, sc in next 7 chs, skip next ch, sc in next 7 chs, ★ 3 sc in next ch, sc in next 7 chs, skip next ch, sc in next 7 chs; repeat from ★ once **more**, 2 sc in last ch: 52 sc.

Note: Loop a short piece of yarn around any stitch to mark Row 1 as **right** side.

Row 2: Ch 1, turn; 2 sc in first sc, sc in next 7 sc, skip next 2 sc, sc in next 7 sc, ★ 3 sc in next sc, sc in next 7 sc, skip next 2 sc, sc in next 7 sc; repeat from ★ once **more**, 2 sc in last sc.

Repeat Row 2 until Dishcloth measures approximately 9¹/₂" from point to point, ending by working a **right** side row; do **not** finish off.

Edging: Ch 1, do **not** turn; sc evenly around entire Dishcloth increasing and decreasing as necessary to keep piece lying flat; join with slip st to first sc, finish off.

55

STITCH GUIDE
BEGINNING CLUSTER (uses next 3 sts)
Ch 2, ★ YO, insert hook in **next** st, YO and pull up a loop, YO and draw through 2 loops on hook; repeat from ★ 2 times **more**, YO and draw through all 4 loops on hook.

CLUSTER (uses next 4 sts)
★ YO, insert hook in **next** st, YO and pull up a loop, YO and draw through 2 loops on hook; repeat from ★ 3 times **more**, YO and draw through all 5 loops on hook.

With first color, ch 6; join with slip st to form a ring.

Rnd 1 (Right side)**:** Ch 6, (dc in ring, ch 3) 7 times; join with slip st to third ch of beginning ch-6: 8 ch-3 sps.

Note: Loop a short piece of yarn around any stitch to mark Rnd 1 as **right** side.

Rnd 2: Ch 3, 4 dc in next ch-3 sp, (dc in next dc, 4 dc in next ch-3 sp) around; join with slip st to top of beginning ch-3: 40 sts.

Rnd 3: Slip st in next dc, ch 3, hdc in next 2 dc, dc in next dc, ch 5, skip next dc, ★ dc in next dc, hdc in next 2 dc, dc in next dc, ch 5, skip next st; repeat from ★ around; join with slip st to top of beginning ch-3, finish off: 8 ch-5 sps.

Rnd 4: With **right** side facing, join next color with slip st in same st as joining; work Beginning Cluster, ch 5, sc in next ch-5 sp, ch 5, ★ work Cluster, ch 5, sc in next ch-5 sp, ch 5; repeat from ★ around; join with slip st to top of Beginning Cluster: 8 Clusters and 16 ch-5 sps.

Rnd 5: Ch 7, hdc in next ch-5 sp, hdc in next sc and in next ch-5 sp, ch 5, ★ hdc in next Cluster, ch 5, hdc in next ch-5 sp, hdc in next sc and in next ch-5 sp, ch 5; repeat from ★ around; join with slip st to second ch of beginning ch-7: 32 sts and 16 ch-5 sps.

Rnd 6: Ch 3, 2 dc in same st, ch 2, dc in next ch-5 sp, ch 2, skip next hdc, ★ (3 dc in next hdc, ch 2, dc in next ch-5 sp, ch 2) twice, skip next hdc; repeat from ★ 6 times **more**, 3 dc in next hdc, ch 2, dc in next ch-5 sp, ch 2; join with slip st to top of beginning ch-3: 64 sts and 32 ch-2 sps.

Rnd 7: Ch 1, sc in same st, ch 5, skip next dc, sc in next dc, ch 3, (sc, ch 3) twice in next dc, ★ sc in next dc, ch 5, skip next dc, sc in next dc, ch 3, (sc, ch 3) twice in next dc; repeat from ★ around; join with slip st to first sc: 64 sc.

Rnd 8: Slip st in first ch-5 sp, ch 1, sc in same sp, ch 3, (sc in next ch-3 sp, ch 3) 3 times, ★ sc in next ch-5 sp, ch 3, (sc in next ch-3 sp, ch 3) 3 times; repeat from ★ around; join with slip st to first sc, finish off.

Design by Sue Galucki.

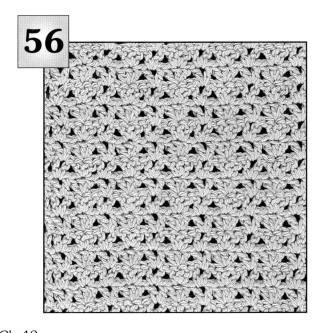

Ch 43.

Row 1 (Right side)**:** (Dc, ch 1, dc) in fifth ch from hook, ★ skip next 2 chs, 3 dc in next ch, skip next 2 chs, (dc, ch 1, dc) in next ch; repeat from ★ across to last 2 chs, skip next ch, dc in last ch: 34 sts and 7 ch-1 sps.

Note: Loop a short piece of yarn around any stitch to mark Row 1 as **right** side.

Row 2: Ch 3 **(counts as first dc)**, turn; (dc, ch 1, dc) in next ch-1 sp, ★ 3 dc in center dc of next 3-dc group, (dc, ch 1, dc) in next ch-1 sp; repeat from ★ across to last dc, skip last dc, dc in next ch.

Repeat Row 2 until Dishcloth measures approximately 10" from beginning ch, ending by working a **right** side row; do **not** finish off.

Work desired Edging, page 58.

Design by Liz Nation.

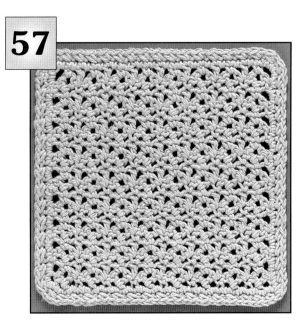

Ch 34.

Row 1 (Wrong side)**:** Sc in second ch from hook, ★ skip next ch, dc in next ch, ch 2, dc around post of dc just made, skip next ch, sc in next ch; repeat from ★ across: 9 sc and 8 ch-2 sps.

Row 2: Ch 4 **(counts as first dc plus ch 1)**, turn; sc in next ch-2 sp, ch 1, skip next dc, dc in next sc, ★ ch 1, sc in next ch-2 sp, ch 1, skip next dc, dc in next sc; repeat from ★ across: 17 sts and 16 ch-1 sps.

Row 3: Ch 1, turn; sc in first dc, ★ dc in next sc, ch 2, dc around post of dc just made, sc in next dc; repeat from ★ across.

Rows 4-18: Repeat Rows 2 and 3, 7 times; then repeat Row 2 once **more**; do **not** finish off.

EDGING
Rnd 1: Ch 1, turn; sc evenly around entire Dishcloth working an even number of sc and working 3 sc in each corner; join with slip st to first sc.

Rnd 2: Ch 1, do **not** turn; sc in next sc, working **loosely** around sc just made, sc in same st as joining, ★ skip next sc, sc in next sc, working **loosely** around sc just made, sc in skipped sc; repeat from ★ around; join with slip st to first sc, finish off.

Design by Valesha Marshell Kirksey.

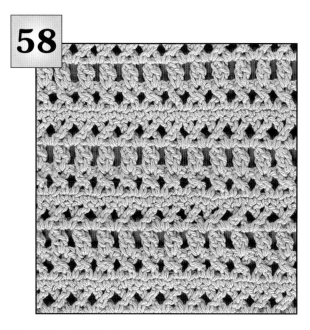

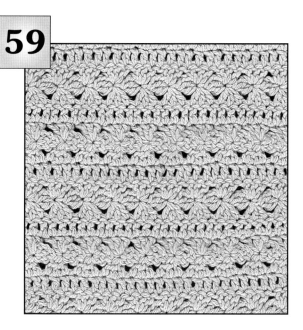

STITCH GUIDE
TREBLE CROCHET *(abbreviated tr)*
YO twice, insert hook in st or sp indicated, YO and pull up a loop (4 loops on hook), (YO and draw through 2 loops on hook) 3 times.

CLUSTER (uses one ch-1 sp)
★ YO, insert hook in ch-1 sp indicated, YO and pull up a loop, YO and draw through 2 loops on hook, YO and draw through one loop on hook; repeat from ★ once **more**, YO and draw through all 3 loops on hook.

———————————————————

Ch 45.

Row 1 (Right side)**:** Sc in second ch from hook and in each ch across: 44 sc.

Note: Loop a short piece of yarn around any stitch to mark Row 1 as **right** side.

Row 2: Ch 3 **(counts as first dc, now and throughout)**, turn; ★ skip next 2 sc, tr in next sc, ch 1, working in **front** of tr just made, tr in first skipped sc **(Cross St made)**; repeat from ★ across to last sc, dc in last sc: 30 sts and 14 ch-1 sps.

Row 3: Ch 5 **(counts as first tr plus ch 1)**, turn; work Cluster in next ch-1 sp, (ch 2, work Cluster in next ch-1 sp) across to last 2 sts, ch 1, skip next tr, tr in last dc: 14 Clusters and 15 sps.

Row 4: Ch 3, turn; skip first ch-1 sp, tr in next ch-2 sp, ch 1, working **behind** tr just made, tr in skipped ch-1 sp **(Cross St made)**, ★ tr in next sp, ch 1, working **behind** tr just made, tr in same sp as first tr of previous Cross St; repeat from ★ across to last tr, dc in last tr: 30 sts and 14 ch-1 sps.

Row 5: Ch 1, turn; sc in each st and in each ch-1 sp across: 44 sc.

Rows 6-17: Repeat Rows 2-5, 3 times; do **not** finish off.

Work desired Edging, page 58.

Design by Valesha Marshell Kirksey.

STITCH GUIDE
DECREASE (uses next 3 sts)
★ YO, insert hook in **next** st, YO and pull up a loop, YO and draw through 2 loops on hook; repeat from ★ 2 times **more**, YO and draw through all 4 loops on hook.

CLUSTER (uses one ch)
★ YO, insert hook in ch indicated, YO and pull up a loop, YO and draw through 2 loops on hook; repeat from ★ once **more**, YO and draw through all 3 loops on hook.

———————————————————

Ch 39.

Row 1 (Right side)**:** Skip first 5 chs, decrease, ★ ch 4, work Cluster in fourth ch from hook, decrease; repeat from ★ across to last ch, ch 2, dc in last ch: 22 sts and 2 sps.

Note: Loop a short piece of yarn around any stitch to mark Row 1 as **right** side.

Row 2: Ch 3 **(counts as first dc, now and throughout)**, turn; skip next ch, 3 dc in next ch, (skip next st and next 3 chs, 3 dc in next ch) across to last st, skip last st and next 2 chs, dc in next ch: 35 dc.

Row 3: Ch 3, turn; dc in next dc and in each dc across.

Row 4: Ch 5, turn; decrease, ★ ch 4, work Cluster in fourth ch from hook, decrease; repeat from ★ across to last dc, ch 2, dc in last dc: 22 sts and 2 sps.

Repeat Rows 2-4 until Dishcloth measures approximately 10" from beginning ch, ending by working Row 2; do **not** finish off.

Work desired Edging, page 58.

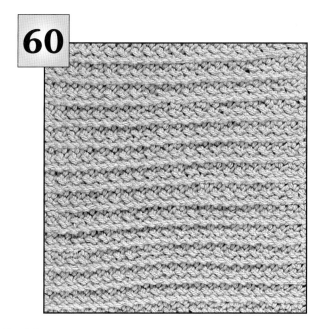

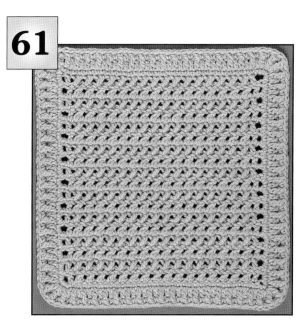

Ch 46.

Row 1 (Right side)**:** Working in back ridges of beginning ch *(Fig. 1, page 2)*, sc in second ch from hook, ★ ch 1, skip next ch, sc in next ch; repeat from ★ across: 23 sc.

Rows 2-28: Ch 1, turn; working in Back Loops Only *(Fig. 2, page 2)*, sc in first sc, (ch 1, sc in next sc) across; do **not** finish off.

EDGING

Rnd 1: Ch 1, turn; working in Back Loops Only, sc in first sc, ch 1, (sc in next sc, ch 1) across; (sc, ch 1) evenly across end of rows; working in Back Loops Only of beginning ch, sc in first ch, ch 1, ★ skip next ch, sc in next ch, ch 1; repeat from ★ across; (sc, ch 1) evenly across end of rows; join with slip st to **both** loops of first sc.

Rnd 2: Ch 1, do **not** turn; working in both loops, sc in same st, ch 1, (sc in next sc, ch 1) around; join with slip st to first sc, finish off.

Design by Valesha Marshell Kirksey.

STITCH GUIDE
TREBLE CROCHET *(abbreviated tr)*
YO twice, working in **front** of ch-1 indicated, insert hook in st indicated, YO and pull up a loop (4 loops on hook), (YO and draw through 2 loops on hook) 3 times.

Ch 38.

Row 1 (Wrong side)**:** Dc in fourth ch from hook **(3 skipped chs count as first dc)**, ★ skip next ch, dc in next ch, working **behind** dc just made, dc in skipped ch; repeat from ★ across to last 2 chs, dc in last 2 chs: 36 dc.

Rows 2-18: Ch 3 **(counts as first dc)**, turn; dc in next dc, ★ skip next dc, dc in next dc, working **behind** dc just made, dc in skipped dc; repeat from ★ across to last 2 dc, dc in last 2 dc; do **not** finish off.

EDGING

Rnd 1: Ch 1, do **not** turn; 2 sc in same st, work 35 sc evenly spaced across to next corner, ★ 3 sc in corner, work 35 sc evenly spaced across to next corner; repeat from ★ 2 times **more**, sc in same st as first sc; join with slip st to first sc: 152 sc.

Rnd 2: Ch 4, (dc in same st, ch 1) twice, ★ skip next sc, (dc in next sc, ch 1, skip next sc) across to center sc of next corner 3-sc group, (dc, ch 1) 3 times in center sc; repeat from ★ 2 times **more**, skip next sc, (dc in next sc, ch 1, skip next sc) across; join with slip st to third ch of beginning ch-4: 84 ch-1 sps.

Rnd 3: Ch 1, sc in same st, tr in corner sc on Rnd 1 **below** next ch-1, sc in next dc, tr in same st on Rnd 1 as last tr, sc in next dc, ★ (tr in skipped sc on Rnd 1 **below** next ch-1, sc in next dc) 19 times, tr in corner sc on Rnd 1 **below** next ch-1, sc in next dc, tr in same st on Rnd 1 as last tr, sc in next dc; repeat from ★ 2 times **more**, tr in skipped sc on Rnd 1 **below** next ch-1, (sc in next dc, tr in skipped sc on Rnd 1 **below** next ch-1) across; join with slip st to first sc, finish off.

Design by Valesha Marshell Kirksey.

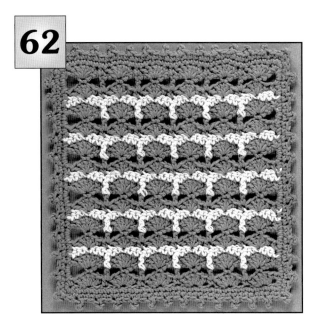

STITCH GUIDE
TREBLE CROCHET *(abbreviated tr)*
YO twice, insert hook around post of dc indicated, YO and pull up a loop (4 loops on hook), (YO and draw through 2 loops on hook) 3 times.

With first color, ch 38.

Row 1 (Right side)**:** Sc in second ch from hook, ★ skip next 2 chs, 5 dc in next ch, skip next 2 chs, sc in next ch; repeat from ★ across: 37 sts.

Row 2: Ch 6 **(counts as first dc plus ch 3)**, turn; skip next 2 dc, sc in next dc, ch 3, skip next 2 dc, dc in next sc, ★ ch 3, skip next 2 dc, sc in next dc, ch 3, skip next 2 dc, dc in next sc; repeat from ★ across: 7 dc and 6 sc.

Row 3: Ch 1, turn; sc in first dc, (5 dc in next sc, sc in next dc) across changing to next color in last sc *(Fig. 3a, page 2)*: 37 sts.

Row 4: Ch 1, turn; sc in first sc and in next 5 dc, ★ working **behind** next sc, tr from **back** to **front** around post of dc one row **below** *(Fig. 4, page 2)*, sc in next 5 dc; repeat from ★ across to last sc, sc in last sc changing to next color.

Row 5: Ch 1, turn; sc in first sc, skip next 2 sc, 5 dc in next sc, skip next 2 sc, ★ sc in next tr, skip next 2 sc, 5 dc in next sc, skip next 2 sc; repeat from ★ across to last sc, sc in last sc.

Rows 6-23: Repeat Rows 2-5, 4 times; then repeat Rows 2 and 3 once **more**; do **not** finish off.

EDGING
Rnd 1: Ch 1, do **not** turn; ★ work 33 sc evenly spaced across to next corner, 3 sc in corner, work 36 sc evenly spaced across to next corner, 3 sc in corner; repeat from ★ once **more**; join with slip st to first sc: 150 sc.

Rnd 2: Ch 1, sc in same st and in next sc, ch 3, slip st in top of last sc made, ★ sc in next 3 sc, ch 3, slip st in top of last sc made; repeat from ★ around to last sc, sc in last sc; join with slip st to first sc, finish off.

Design by Frances Moore-Kyle.

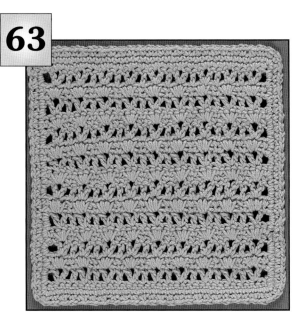

STITCH GUIDE
LONG SINGLE CROCHET *(abbreviated LSC)*
Working around ch-3, insert hook in ch-1 sp indicated, YO and pull up a loop even with last st made, YO and draw through both loops on hook **(counts as one sc)**.

DECREASE
Pull up a loop in next 2 sc, YO and draw through all 3 loops on hook.

Ch 38.

Row 1: Sc in second ch from hook and in each ch across: 37 sc.

Row 2 (Right side)**:** Ch 3 **(counts as first dc, now and throughout)**, turn; ★ skip next sc, (dc, ch 1, dc) in next sc, skip next sc, dc in next sc; repeat from ★ across: 28 dc and 9 ch-1 sps.

Row 3: Ch 1, turn; sc in first dc, ★ ch 3, skip next 2 dc, sc in next dc; repeat from ★ across: 10 sc and 9 ch-3 sps.

Row 4: Ch 1, turn; sc in first sc, ★ work 3 LSC in ch-1 sp one row **below** next ch-3, sc in next sc; repeat from ★ across: 37 sts.

Rows 5-23: Repeat Rows 2-4, 6 times; then repeat Row 2 once **more**.

Row 24: Ch 1, turn; sc in each dc and in each ch-1 sp across; do **not** finish off: 37 sc.

EDGING
Rnd 1: Ch 1, do **not** turn; sc evenly around entire Dishcloth working a number of sc that is divisible by 3 and working 3 sc in each corner; join with slip st to first sc.

Rnd 2: Ch 1, sc in same st, ch 1, decrease, ch 1, ★ sc in next sc, ch 1, decrease, ch 1; repeat from ★ around; join with slip st to first sc, finish off.

Design by Valesha Marshell Kirksey.

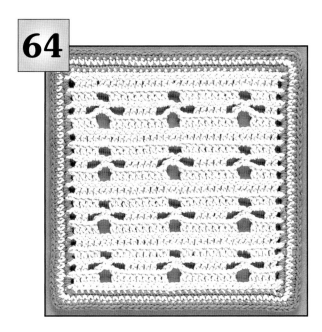

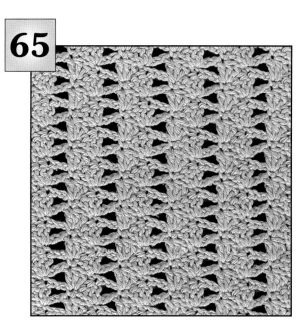

With first color, ch 35.

Row 1: Sc in second ch from hook and in each ch across: 34 sc.

Row 2 (Right side)**:** Ch 3 **(counts as first dc, now and throughout)**, turn; dc in next 4 sc, ch 4, skip next 2 sc, ★ dc in next 9 sc, ch 4, skip next 2 sc; repeat from ★ once **more**, dc in last 5 sc: 28 dc.

Note: Loop a short piece of yarn around any stitch to mark Row 2 as **right** side.

Row 3: Ch 3, turn; dc in next 2 dc, ch 3, sc in next ch-4 sp, ch 3, ★ skip next 2 dc, dc in next 5 dc, ch 3, sc in next ch-4 sp, ch 3; repeat from ★ once **more**, skip next 2 dc, dc in last 3 dc: 16 dc.

Row 4: Ch 3, turn; dc in next 2 dc, 2 dc in next ch-3 sp, ch 2, 2 dc in next ch-3 sp, ★ dc in next 5 dc, 2 dc in next ch-3 sp, ch 2, 2 dc in next ch-3 sp; repeat from ★ once **more**, dc in last 3 dc: 28 dc.

Row 5: Ch 3, turn; dc in next 4 dc, 2 dc in next ch-2 sp, (dc in next 9 dc, 2 dc in next ch-2 sp) twice, dc in last 5 dc: 34 dc.

Row 6: Ch 3, turn; dc in next 4 dc, ch 4, skip next 2 dc, ★ dc in next 9 dc, ch 4, skip next 2 dc; repeat from ★ once **more**, dc in last 5 dc: 28 dc.

Rows 7-17: Repeat Rows 3-6 twice, then repeat Rows 3-5 once **more**.

Row 18: Ch 1, turn; sc in each dc across; finish off.

EDGING
Rnd 1: With **right** side facing, join next color with slip st in any st; ch 1, sc evenly around entire Dishcloth working 3 sc in each corner; join with slip st to first sc, finish off.

Rnds 2 and 3: With **right** side facing, join next color with slip st in any sc; ch 1, sc in same st and in each sc around working 3 sc in center sc of each corner; join with slip st to first sc, finish off.

Design by Rosetta Harshman.

Ch 40.

Row 1 (Right side)**:** Sc in second ch from hook, skip next 2 chs, 3 dc in next ch, ★ ch 3, skip next 3 chs, sc in next ch, skip next 2 chs, 3 dc in next ch; repeat from ★ across: 24 sts and 5 ch-3 sps.

Note: Loop a short piece of yarn around any stitch to mark Row 1 as **right** side.

Row 2: Ch 1, turn; sc in first dc, skip next 2 dc, 3 dc in next sc, ★ ch 3, sc in next dc, skip next 2 dc, 3 dc in next sc; repeat from ★ across.

Repeat Row 2 until Dishcloth measures approximately 9" from beginning ch; do **not** finish off.

Work desired Edging, page 58.

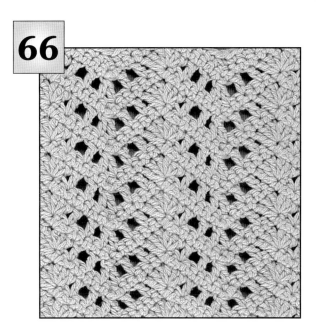

66

STITCH GUIDE
SC DECREASE (uses next 3 sts)
Pull up a loop in next ch, skip next st, pull up a loop in next ch, YO and draw through all 3 loops on hook.

DC DECREASE (uses next 3 sts)
† YO, insert hook in **next** sc, YO and pull up a loop, YO and draw through 2 loops on hook †, skip next st, repeat from † to † once, YO and draw through all 3 loops on hook.

Ch 44.

Row 1: Pull up a loop in second and third ch from hook, YO and draw through all 3 loops on hook, sc in next 5 chs, 3 sc in next ch, sc in next 5 chs, ★ sc decrease, sc in next 5 chs, 3 sc in next ch, sc in next 5 chs; repeat from ★ once **more**, pull up a loop in last 2 chs, YO and draw through all 3 loops on hook: 43 sts.

Row 2 (Right side)**:** Ch 2, turn; dc in next sc **(beginning dc decrease made)**, (ch 1, skip next sc, dc in next sc) twice, skip next sc, (3 dc, ch 1, 3 dc) in next sc, skip next sc, (dc in next sc, ch 1, skip next sc) twice, ★ dc decrease, (ch 1, skip next sc, dc in next sc) twice, skip next sc, (3 dc, ch 1, 3 dc) in next sc, skip next sc, (dc in next sc, ch 1, skip next sc) twice; repeat from ★ once **more**, † YO, insert hook in **next** st, YO and pull up a loop, YO and draw through 2 loops on hook †, repeat from † to † once **more**, YO and draw through all 3 loops on hook **(ending dc decrease made)**: 34 sts and 15 ch-1 sps.

Row 3: Ch 1, turn; pull up a loop in first st and in next ch, YO and draw through all 3 loops on hook **(beginning sc decrease made)**, sc in next dc and in next ch, sc in next 3 dc, 3 sc in next ch-1 sp, skip next dc, sc in next 3 dc and in next ch, sc in next dc, ★ sc decrease, sc in next dc and in next ch, sc in next 3 dc, 3 sc in next ch-1 sp, skip next dc, sc in next 3 dc and in next ch, sc in next dc; repeat from ★ once **more**, pull up a loop in next ch and in last st, YO and draw through all 3 loops on hook **(ending sc decrease made)**: 43 sts.

Rows 4-19: Repeat Rows 2 and 3, 8 times; do **not** finish off.

Edging: Ch 1, turn; sc evenly around entire Dishcloth increasing and decreasing as necessary to keep piece lying flat; join with slip st to first sc, finish off.

Design by Jennine Korejko.

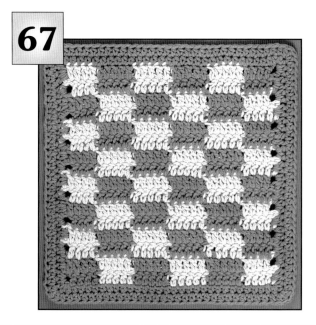

67

Note: Do **not** cut yarn unless specified. Work over color not being used, holding it with normal tension and keeping yarn to **wrong** side.

With first color, ch 32.

Row 1: Dc in fourth ch from hook **(3 skipped chs count as first dc)** and in next 3 chs changing to second color in last dc made *(Fig. 3b, page 2)*, (dc in next 5 chs changing to first color in last dc made, dc in next 5 chs changing to second color in last dc made) twice, dc in last 5 chs: 30 dc.

Row 2 (Right side)**:** Ch 3 **(counts as first dc, now and throughout)**, turn; dc in next 4 dc, with first color dc in next 5 dc, (with second color dc in next 5 dc, with first color dc in next 5 dc) twice changing to second color in last dc.

Row 3: Ch 3, turn; dc in next 4 dc, with first color dc in next 5 dc, (with second color dc in next 5 dc, with first color dc in next 5 dc) twice.

Row 4: Ch 3, turn; dc in next 4 dc, with second color dc in next 5 dc, (with first color dc in next 5 dc, with second color dc in next 5 dc) twice changing to first color in last dc.

Row 5: Ch 3, turn; dc in next 4 dc, with second color dc in next 5 dc, (with first color dc in next 5 dc, with second color dc in next 5 dc) twice.

Row 6: Ch 3, turn; dc in next 4 dc, with first color dc in next 5 dc, (with second color dc in next 5 dc, with first color dc in next 5 dc) twice changing to second color in last dc.

Rows 7-16: Repeat Rows 3-6 twice, then repeat Rows 3 and 4 once **more**; at end of Row 16, cut second color; do **not** finish off first color.

EDGING

Rnd 1: Do **not** turn; slip st in end of first row, ch 2, hdc evenly around entire Dishcloth working 3 hdc in each corner; join with slip st to top of beginning ch-2.

Rnd 2: Ch 2, hdc in next hdc and in each hdc around working 3 hdc in center hdc of each corner; join with slip st to top of beginning ch-2, finish off.

Design by Rosetta Harshman.

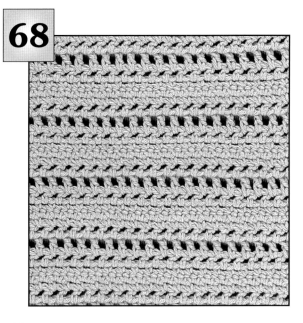

Ch 42.

Row 1 (Right side)**:** Sc in second ch from hook, ★ ch 1, skip next ch, sc in next ch; repeat from ★ across: 21 sc and 20 ch-1 sps.

Note: Loop a short piece of yarn around any stitch to mark Row 1 as **right** side.

Row 2: Ch 2 **(counts as first hdc, now and throughout)**, turn; hdc in next ch-1 sp, (ch 1, hdc in next ch-1 sp) across to last sc, hdc in last sc: 19 ch-1 sps.

Row 3: Ch 4 **(counts as first dc plus ch 1)**, turn; (dc in next ch-1 sp, ch 1) across to last 2 hdc, skip next hdc, dc in last hdc: 20 ch-1 sps.

Row 4: Ch 2, turn; hdc in next ch-1 sp, (ch 1, hdc in next ch-1 sp) across to last dc, hdc in last dc: 19 ch-1 sps.

Row 5: Ch 1, turn; sc in first hdc, ch 1, (sc in next ch-1 sp, ch 1) across to last 2 hdc, skip next hdc, sc in last hdc: 20 ch-1 sps.

Row 6: Ch 1, turn; sc in each sc and in each ch-1 sp across: 41 sc.

Row 7: Ch 1, turn; sc in first sc, ★ ch 1, skip next sc, sc in next sc; repeat from ★ across: 20 ch-1 sps.

Rows 8-29: Repeat Rows 2-7, 3 times; then repeat Rows 2-5 once **more**; do **not** finish off: 20 ch-1 sps.

Work desired Edging, page 58.

Design by Patty Kowaleski.

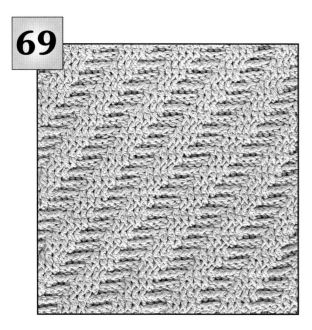

69

STITCH GUIDE
BACK POST DOUBLE CROCHET
(abbreviated BPdc)
YO, insert hook from **back** to **front** around post of st indicated *(Fig. 4, page 2)*, YO and pull up a loop (3 loops on hook), (YO and draw through 2 loops on hook) twice.

FRONT POST DOUBLE CROCHET
(abbreviated FPdc)
YO, insert hook from **front** to **back** around post of st indicated *(Fig. 4, page 2)*, YO and pull up a loop (3 loops on hook), (YO and draw through 2 loops on hook) twice.

Ch 44.

Row 1: Dc in fourth ch from hook **(3 skipped chs count as first dc)** and in each ch across: 42 dc.

Row 2 (Right side)**:** Ch 2 **(counts as first hdc, now and throughout)**, turn; ★ work FPdc around each of next 4 dc, work BPdc around each of next 4 dc; repeat from ★ across to last dc, hdc in last dc.

Note: Loop a short piece of yarn around any stitch to mark Row 2 as **right** side.

Row 3: Ch 2, turn; work BPdc around next BPdc, work FPdc around each of next 4 sts, ★ work BPdc around each of next 4 sts, work FPdc around each of next 4 sts; repeat from ★ across to last 4 sts, work BPdc around each of next 3 FPdc, hdc in last hdc.

Row 4: Ch 2, turn; work FPdc around each of next 2 BPdc, work BPdc around each of next 4 sts, ★ work FPdc around each of next 4 sts, work BPdc around each of next 4 sts; repeat from ★ across to last 3 sts, work FPdc around each of next 2 sts, hdc in last hdc.

Row 5: Ch 2, turn; work BPdc around each of next 3 sts, work FPdc around each of next 4 sts, ★ work BPdc around each of next 4 sts, work FPdc around each of next 4 sts; repeat from ★ across to last 2 sts, work BPdc around next FPdc, hdc in last hdc.

Row 6: Ch 2, turn; ★ work BPdc around each of next 4 sts, work FPdc around each of next 4 sts; repeat from ★ across to last hdc, hdc in last hdc.

Row 7: Ch 2, turn; work FPdc around next FPdc, work BPdc around each of next 4 sts, ★ work FPdc around each of next 4 sts, work BPdc around each of next 4 sts; repeat from ★ across to last 4 sts, work FPdc around each of next 3 BPdc, hdc in last hdc.

Row 8: Ch 2, turn; work BPdc around each of next 2 FPdc, work FPdc around each of next 4 sts, ★ work BPdc around each of next 4 sts, work FPdc around each of next 4 sts; repeat from ★ across to last 3 sts, work BPdc around each of next 2 sts, hdc in last hdc.

Row 9: Ch 2, turn; work FPdc around each of next 3 sts, work BPdc around each of next 4 sts, ★ work FPdc around each of next 4 sts, work BPdc around each of next 4 sts; repeat from ★ across to last 2 sts, work FPdc around next BPdc, hdc in last hdc.

Row 10: Ch 2, turn; ★ work FPdc around each of next 4 sts, work BPdc around each of next 4 sts; repeat from ★ across to last hdc, hdc in last hdc.

Repeat Rows 3-10 until Dishcloth measures approximately 10" from beginning ch; do **not** finish off.

Work desired Edging, page 58.

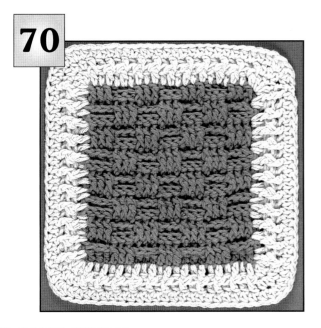

70

STITCH GUIDE
FRONT POST DOUBLE CROCHET
(abbreviated FPdc)
YO, insert hook from **front** to **back** around post of st indicated *(Fig. 4, page 2)*, YO and pull up a loop (3 loops on hook), (YO and draw through 2 loops on hook) twice.

BACK POST DOUBLE CROCHET
(abbreviated BPdc)
YO, insert hook from **back** to **front** around post of st indicated *(Fig. 4, page 2)*, YO and pull up a loop (3 loops on hook), (YO and draw through 2 loops on hook) twice.

With first color, ch 25.

Row 1 (Right side)**:** Dc in fourth ch from hook **(3 skipped chs count as first dc)** and in each ch across: 23 dc.

Note: Loop a short piece of yarn around any stitch to mark Row 1 as **right** side.

Row 2: Ch 2 **(counts as first hdc, now and throughout)**, turn; work FPdc around each of next 3 dc, ★ work BPdc around each of next 3 dc, work FPdc around each of next 3 dc; repeat from ★ 2 times **more**, hdc in last dc.

Row 3: Ch 2, turn; work FPdc around each of next 3 FPdc, ★ work BPdc around each of next 3 BPdc, work FPdc around each of next 3 FPdc; repeat from ★ 2 times **more**, hdc in last hdc.

Row 4: Ch 2, turn; work BPdc around each of next 3 FPdc, ★ work FPdc around each of next 3 BPdc, work BPdc around each of next 3 FPdc; repeat from ★ 2 times **more**, hdc in last hdc.

Row 5: Ch 2, turn; work BPdc around each of next 3 BPdc, ★ work FPdc around each of next 3 FPdc, work BPdc around each of next 3 BPdc; repeat from ★ 2 times **more**, hdc in last hdc.

Row 6: Ch 2, turn; work BPdc around each of next 3 BPdc, ★ work BPdc around each of next 3 FPdc, work FPdc around each of next 3 BPdc; repeat from ★ 2 times **more**, hdc in last hdc.

Rows 7-15: Repeat Rows 3-6 twice, then repeat Row 3 once **more**.

Finish off.

EDGING
Rnd 1: With **right** side facing, join next color with slip st in first hdc on Row 15; ch 3, 2 dc in same st, dc in each st across to last hdc, 3 dc in last hdc; work 21 dc evenly spaced across end of rows; working in free loops of beginning ch *(Fig. 5, page 2)*, 3 dc in first ch, dc in next 21 chs, 3 dc in next ch; work 21 dc evenly spaced across end of rows; join with slip st to top of beginning ch-3: 96 sts.

Rnd 2: Ch 2, do **not** turn; 2 hdc in next dc, hdc in next dc, ★ † work FPdc around next dc, (work BPdc around next dc, work FPdc around next dc) 10 times †, hdc in next dc, 2 hdc in next dc, hdc in next dc; repeat from ★ 2 times **more**, then repeat from † to † once; join with slip st to first hdc: 100 sts.

Rnd 3: Ch 2, 2 hdc in each of next 2 hdc, ★ hdc in next 23 sts, 2 hdc in each of next 2 hdc; repeat from ★ 2 times **more**, hdc in each st across; join with slip st to first hdc, finish off.

Design by Rosetta Harshman.

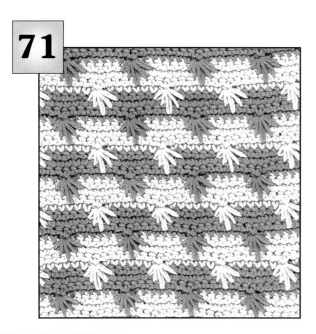

71

STITCH GUIDE
CLUSTER
Working **below** next sc, insert hook in sc one row **below** and 2 sc to the **right** *(Fig. 11a)*, YO and pull up a loop even with loop on hook, insert hook in sc 2 rows **below** and one sc to the **right**, YO and pull up a loop even with loop on hook, insert hook in sc 3 rows **below**, YO and pull up a loop even with loop on hook, insert hook in sc 2 rows **below** and one sc to the **left**, YO and pull up a loop even with loop on hook, insert hook in sc one row **below** and 2 sc to the **left**, YO and pull up a loop even with loop on hook, YO and draw through all 6 loops on hook *(Fig. 11b)*.

Fig. 11a

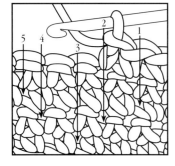

Fig. 11b

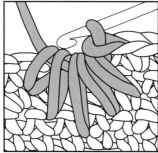

With first color, ch 42.

Row 1 (Right side)**:** Sc in second ch from hook and in each ch across: 41 sc.

Note: Loop a short piece of yarn around any stitch to mark Row 1 as **right** side.

Rows 2-4: Ch 1, turn; sc in each st across changing to next color in last sc on last row *(Fig. 3a, page 2)*.

Row 5: Ch 1, turn; sc in first 4 sc, work Cluster, (sc in next 7 sc, work Cluster) across to last 4 sc, sc in last 4 sc: 36 sc and 5 Clusters.

Rows 6-8: Ch 1, turn; sc in each st across changing to next color in last sc on last row.

Row 9: Ch 1, turn; sc in first 8 sc, work Cluster, (sc in next 7 sc, work Cluster) 3 times, sc in last 8 sc: 37 sc and 4 Clusters.

Repeat Rows 2-9 until Dishcloth measures approximately 10" from beginning ch, ending by working Row 4; do **not** change colors at end of last row and do **not** finish off.

Work desired Edging, page 58.

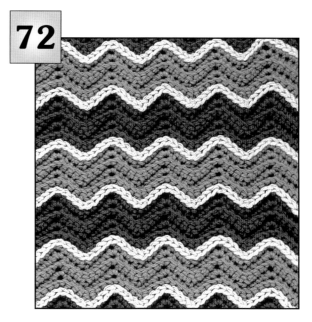

72

STITCH GUIDE
BEGINNING DECREASE
Pull up a loop in first 2 sts, YO and draw through all 3 loops on hook.

DECREASE
Pull up a loop in next 2 sts, YO and draw through all 3 loops on hook.

With first color, ch 48.

Row 1 (Wrong side)**:** Sc in second ch from hook and in next 4 chs, 3 sc in next ch, ★ sc in next 3 chs, skip next 2 chs, sc in next 3 chs, 3 sc in next ch; repeat from ★ across to last 5 chs, sc in last 5 chs: 49 sc.

Row 2: Ch 1, turn; working in Back Loops Only *(Fig. 2, page 2)*, work beginning decrease, sc in next 4 sc, 3 sc in next sc, ★ sc in next 3 sc, skip next 2 sc, sc in next 3 sc, 3 sc in next sc; repeat from ★ across to last 6 sts, sc in next 4 sc, decrease.

Row 3: Ch 1, turn; working in Back Loops Only, work beginning decrease, sc in next 4 sc, 3 sc in next sc, ★ sc in next 3 sc, skip next 2 sc, sc in next 3 sc, 3 sc in next sc; repeat from ★ across to last 6 sts, sc in next 4 sc, decrease changing to next color *(Fig. 3a, page 2)*.

Row 4: Ch 1, turn; slip st **loosely** in **both** loops of each st across changing to next color in last slip st.

41

Row 5: Ch 1, turn; working in Back Loops Only of same sts as slip sts, work beginning decrease, sc in next 4 sc, 3 sc in next sc, ★ sc in next 3 sc, skip next 2 sc, sc in next 3 sc, 3 sc in next sc; repeat from ★ across to last 6 sts, sc in next 4 sc, decrease.

Rows 6-9: Ch 1, turn; working in Back Loops Only, work beginning decrease, sc in next 4 sc, 3 sc in next sc, ★ sc in next 3 sc, skip next 2 sc, sc in next 3 sc, 3 sc in next sc; repeat from ★ across to last 6 sts, sc in next 4 sc, decrease changing to next color in last decrease on last row.

Rows 10-37: Repeat Rows 4-9, 4 times; then repeat Rows 4-7 once **more**.

Edging: Ch 1, turn; sc evenly around entire Dishcloth increasing and decreasing as necessary to keep piece lying flat; join with slip st to first sc, finish off.

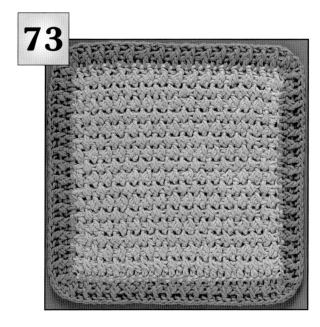

STITCH GUIDE
FRONT POST DOUBLE CROCHET
(abbreviated FPdc)
YO, insert hook from **front** to **back** around post of st indicated *(Fig. 4, page 2)*, YO and pull up a loop (3 loops on hook), (YO and draw through 2 loops on hook) twice.

BACK POST DOUBLE CROCHET
(abbreviated BPdc)
YO, insert hook from **back** to **front** around post of st indicated *(Fig. 4, page 2)*, YO and pull up a loop (3 loops on hook), (YO and draw through 2 loops on hook) twice.

With first color, ch 33.

Row 1 (Right side)**:** Dc in fourth ch from hook **(3 skipped chs count as first st)** and in each ch across: 31 dc.

Note: Loop a short piece of yarn around any stitch to mark Row 1 as **right** side.

Row 2: Ch 2 **(counts as first hdc, now and throughout)**, turn; work FPdc around next st, (work BPdc around next st, work FPdc around next st) across to last st, hdc in last st.

Repeat Row 2 until Dishcloth measures approximately 9" from beginning ch, ending by working a **right** side row.

Finish off.

EDGING
Rnd 1: With **right** side facing, join next color with slip st in first hdc; ch 3, 2 dc in same st, dc in each st across to last hdc, 3 dc in last hdc; work 29 dc evenly spaced across end of rows; working in free loops of beginning ch *(Fig. 5, page 2)*, 3 dc in first ch, dc in next 29 chs, 3 dc in next ch; work 29 dc evenly spaced across end of rows; join with slip st to top of beginning ch-3: 128 sts.

Rnd 2: Slip st in next dc, ch 2, 2 hdc in same st, ★ work FPdc around next dc, (work BPdc around next dc, work FPdc around next dc) across to center dc of next corner 3-dc group, 3 hdc in center dc; repeat from ★ 2 times **more**, work FPdc around next dc, (work BPdc around next dc, work FPdc around next dc) across; join with slip st to first hdc, finish off.

Design by Rhona Czepiel.

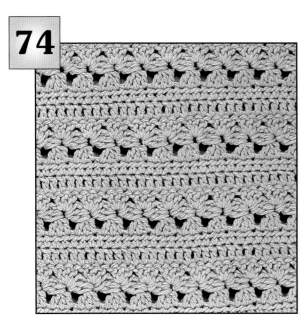

STITCH GUIDE

CLUSTER (uses one st)
Ch 3, ★ YO, insert hook in st indicated, YO and pull up a loop, YO and draw through 2 loops on hook; repeat from ★ once **more**, YO and draw through 3 loops on hook.

DECREASE (uses next 3 hdc)
★ YO, insert hook in **next** hdc, YO and pull up a loop, YO and draw through 2 loops on hook; repeat from ★ 2 times **more**, YO and draw through all 4 loops on hook.

ENDING DECREASE (uses last 2 hdc)
★ YO, insert hook in **next** hdc, YO and pull up a loop, YO and draw through 2 loops on hook; repeat from ★ once **more**, YO and draw through all 3 loops on hook.

Ch 39.

Row 1 (Right side)**:** Dc in fourth ch from hook **(3 skipped chs count as first dc)** and in each ch across: 37 dc.

Note: Loop a short piece of yarn around any stitch to mark Row 1 as **right** side.

Row 2: Ch 2 **(counts as first hdc, now and throughout)**, turn; hdc in next dc and in each dc across.

Row 3: Ch 3 **(counts as first dc, now and throughout)**, turn; dc in same st, work Cluster in top of last dc made, skip next hdc, (decrease, work Cluster in top of last decrease made) across to last 2 hdc, work ending decrease: 26 sts.

Row 4: Ch 3, turn; dc in same st, (skip next Cluster, 3 dc in next decrease) across to last Cluster, skip last Cluster and next dc, 2 dc in last dc: 37 dc.

Row 5: Ch 3, turn; dc in next dc and in each dc across.

Row 6: Ch 2, turn; hdc in next dc and in each dc across.

Repeat Rows 3-6 until Dishcloth measures approximately 10½" from beginning ch, ending by working Row 6; do **not** finish off.

Work desired Edging, page 58.

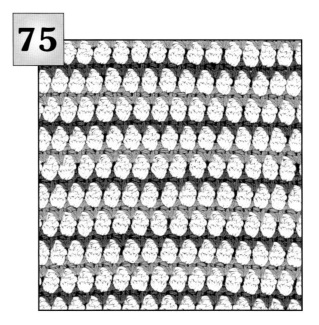

STITCH GUIDE

2-DC CLUSTER (uses one hdc)
★ YO, insert hook in hdc indicated, YO and pull up a loop, YO and draw through 2 loops on hook; repeat from ★ once **more**, YO and draw through all 3 loops on hook.

3-DC CLUSTER (uses one ch-1 sp)
★ YO, insert hook in ch-1 sp indicated, YO and pull up a loop, YO and draw through 2 loops on hook; repeat from ★ 2 times **more**, YO and draw through all 4 loops on hook.

With first color, ch 39.

Row 1 (Right side)**:** Hdc in third ch from hook **(2 skipped chs count as first hdc)**, ★ skip next ch, (hdc, ch 1, hdc) in next ch; repeat from ★ across to last 2 chs, skip next ch, 2 hdc in last ch changing to next color in last hdc *(Fig. 3a, page 2)*: 38 hdc and 17 ch-1 sps.

Note: Loop a short piece of yarn around any stitch to mark Row 1 as **right** side.

Row 2: Ch 3 **(counts as first dc, now and throughout)**, turn; dc in same st, ch 1, (work 3-dc Cluster in next ch-1 sp, ch 1) across to last 3 hdc, skip next 2 hdc, work 2-dc Cluster in last hdc changing to next color: 20 sts and 18 ch-1 sps.

Row 3: Ch 2 **(counts as first hdc, now and throughout)**, turn; (hdc, ch 1, hdc) in each ch-1 sp across to last 2 dc, skip next dc, hdc in last dc changing to next color: 38 hdc and 18 ch-1 sps.

Row 4: Ch 3, turn; work 3-dc Cluster in next ch-1 sp, (ch 1, work 3-dc Cluster in next ch-1 sp) across to last 2 hdc, skip next hdc, dc in last hdc changing to next color: 20 sts and 17 ch-1 sps.

Row 5: Ch 2, turn; hdc in same st, (hdc, ch 1, hdc) in each ch-1 sp across to last 2 sts, skip next 3-dc Cluster, 2 hdc in last dc changing to next color in last hdc: 38 hdc and 17 ch-1 sps.

Repeat Rows 2-5 until Dishcloth measures approximately 11" from beginning ch, ending by working Row 5; do **not** change colors at end of last row and do **not** finish off.

Work desired Edging, page 58.

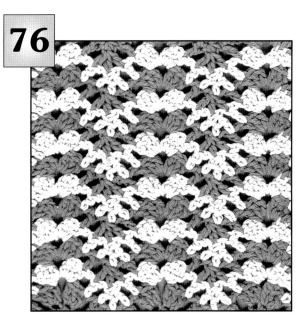

STITCH GUIDE

DECREASE (uses next 3 chs)
★ YO, insert hook in **next** ch, YO and pull up a loop, YO and draw through 2 loops on hook; repeat from ★ 2 times **more**, YO and draw through all 4 loops on hook.

CLUSTER (uses next 5 sts)
YO, insert hook in next dc, YO and pull up a loop, YO and draw through 2 loops on hook, ★ YO, skip **next** ch-1 sp, insert hook in **next** st, YO and pull up a loop, YO and draw through 2 loops on hook; repeat from ★ once **more**, YO and draw through all 4 loops on hook.

With first color, ch 35.

Row 1 (Right side)**:** Dc in third ch from hook, ch 1, skip next ch, dc in next ch, ch 1, skip next ch, 3 dc in next ch, ch 3, 3 dc in next ch, ch 1, skip next ch, dc in next ch, ch 1, ★ skip next ch, decrease, ch 1, skip next ch, dc in next ch, ch 1, skip next ch, 3 dc in next ch, ch 3, 3 dc in next ch, ch 1, skip next ch, dc in next ch, ch 1; repeat from ★ once **more**, skip next ch, dc in next 2 chs changing to next color in last dc *(Fig. 3a, page 2)*: 29 sts and 15 sps.

Note: Loop a short piece of yarn around any stitch to mark Row 1 as **right** side.

Row 2: Ch 2, turn; skip first 2 dc, (dc in next dc, ch 1) twice, (3 dc, ch 3, 3 dc) in next ch-3 sp, ch 1, skip next 2 dc, dc in next dc, ch 1, ★ work Cluster, ch 1, dc in next dc, ch 1, (3 dc, ch 3, 3 dc) in next ch-3 sp, ch 1, skip next 2 dc, dc in next dc, ch 1; repeat from ★ once **more**, skip next dc, dc in last dc changing to next color: 29 sts and 15 sps.

Repeat Row 2 until Dishcloth measures approximately 9" from point to point, ending by working a **right** side row; do **not** change colors at end of last row and do **not** finish off.

Edging: Ch 1, do **not** turn; sc evenly around entire Dishcloth increasing and decreasing as necessary to keep piece lying flat; join with slip st to first sc, finish off.

44

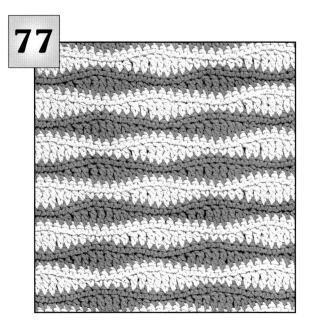

77

STITCH GUIDE
TREBLE CROCHET *(abbreviated tr)*
YO twice, insert hook in st indicated, YO and pull up a loop (4 loops on hook), (YO and draw through 2 loops on hook) 3 times.

With first color, ch 44.

Row 1 (Right side)**:** Sc in second ch from hook and in next ch, hdc in next 2 chs, dc in next 2 chs, tr in next 3 chs, dc in next 2 chs, hdc in next 2 chs, ★ sc in next 3 chs, hdc in next 2 chs, dc in next 2 chs, tr in next 3 chs, dc in next 2 chs, hdc in next 2 chs; repeat from ★ once **more**, sc in last 2 chs: 43 sts.

Note #1: Loop a short piece of yarn around any stitch to mark Row 1 as **right** side.

Note #2: Do **not** cut yarn unless otherwise instructed. Carry unused yarn **loosely** along end of rows.

Row 2: Ch 1, turn; sc in each st across changing to next color in last sc *(Fig. 3a, page 2)*.

Row 3: Ch 4 **(counts as first tr)**, turn; tr in next sc, dc in next 2 sc, hdc in next 2 sc, sc in next 3 sc, hdc in next 2 sc, dc in next 2 sc, ★ tr in next 3 sc, dc in next 2 sc, hdc in next 2 sc, sc in next 3 sc, hdc in next 2 sc, dc in next 2 sc; repeat from ★ once **more**, tr in last 2 sc.

Row 4: Ch 1, turn; sc in each st across changing to next color in last sc.

Row 5: Ch 1, turn; sc in first 2 sc, hdc in next 2 sc, dc in next 2 sc, tr in next 3 sc, dc in next 2 sc, hdc in next 2 sc, ★ sc in next 3 sc, hdc in next 2 sc, dc in next 2 sc, tr in next 3 sc, dc in next 2 sc, hdc in next 2 sc; repeat from ★ once **more**, sc in last 2 sc.

Row 6: Ch 1, turn; sc in each st across changing to next color in last sc.

Repeat Rows 3-6 until Dishcloth measures approximately 11" from beginning ch, ending by working Row 6, do **not** change colors at end of last row, cut previous color; do **not** finish off.

Work desired Edging, page 58.

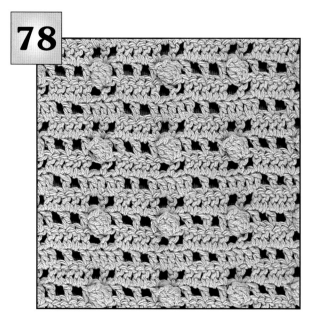

78

STITCH GUIDE
POPCORN
5 Dc in next dc, drop loop from hook, insert hook in first dc of 5-dc group, hook dropped loop and draw through.

Ch 39.

Row 1 (Right side)**:** Dc in fourth ch from hook **(3 skipped chs count as first dc)** and in each ch across: 37 dc.

Note: Loop a short piece of yarn around any stitch to mark Row 1 as **right** side.

Row 2: Ch 3 **(counts as first dc, now and throughout)**, turn; dc in next 4 dc, ★ ch 1, skip next dc, dc in next dc, ch 1, skip next dc, dc in next 5 dc; repeat from ★ across: 29 dc and 8 ch-1 sps.

Row 3: Ch 3, turn; dc in next 4 dc, dc in next ch-1 sp, dc in next dc and in next ch-1 sp, ★ (dc in next dc, ch 1, skip next dc) twice, (dc in next dc and in next ch-1 sp) twice; repeat from ★ 2 times **more**, dc in last 5 dc: 31 dc and 6 ch-1 sps.

Row 4: Ch 3, turn; dc in next 4 dc, ch 1, skip next dc, dc in next dc, ch 1, skip next dc, ★ (dc in next dc and in next ch-1 sp) twice, (dc in next dc, ch 1, skip next dc) twice; repeat from ★ 2 times **more**, dc in last 5 dc: 29 dc and 8 ch-1 sps.

Row 5: Ch 3, turn; dc in next 4 dc, ch 1, work Popcorn in next dc, ch 1, ★ dc in next dc, ch 1, (skip next dc, dc in next dc, ch 1) twice, work Popcorn in next dc, ch 1; repeat from ★ 2 times **more**, dc in last 5 dc: 4 Popcorns and 14 ch-1 sps.

Row 6: Ch 3, turn; dc in next 4 dc, ch 1, dc in next Popcorn, ch 1, ★ dc in next dc, (dc in next ch-1 sp and in next dc) twice, ch 1, dc in next Popcorn, ch 1; repeat from ★ 2 times **more**, dc in last 5 dc: 29 dc and 8 ch-1 sps.

Rows 7-16: Repeat Rows 3-6 twice; then repeat Rows 3 and 4 once **more**.

Row 17: Ch 3, turn; dc in next dc and in each dc and each ch-1 sp across; do **not** finish off.

Work desired Edging, page 58.

Design by Cathy Hardy.

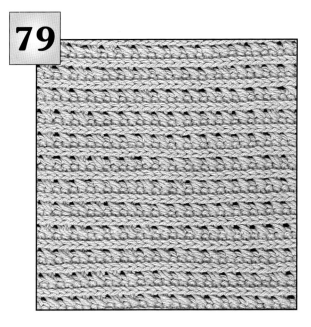

Ch 37.

Row 1 (Wrong side)**:** Sc in second ch from hook and in each ch across: 36 sc.

Note: Loop a short piece of yarn around **back** of any stitch on Row 1 to mark **right** side.

Row 2: Ch 2, turn; hdc in first sc, ★ skip next sc, hdc in next sc, working **loosely** around hdc just made, hdc in skipped sc; repeat from ★ across to last sc, hdc in last sc.

Row 3: Ch 1, turn; sc in horizontal strand *(Fig. 12)* of each hdc across.

Fig. 12

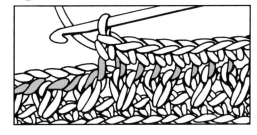

Repeat Rows 2 and 3 until Dishcloth measures approximately 9" from beginning ch, ending by working Row 3; do **not** finish off.

Work desired Edging, page 58.

Design by Darla Sims.

80

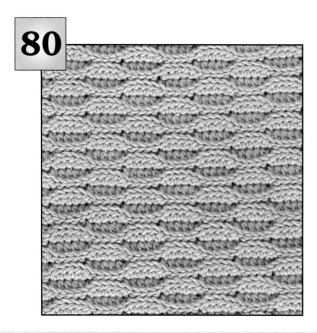

81

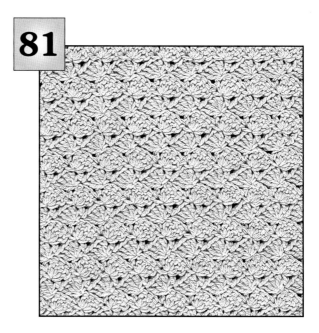

Note: When instructed to slip st, always slip st **loosely**.

Ch 46.

Row 1 (Right side)**:** Slip st in second ch from hook and in next 4 chs, (hdc in next 5 chs, slip st in next 5 chs) across: 45 sts.

Note #1: Loop a short piece of yarn around any stitch to mark Row 1 as **right** side.

Note #2: Work in Back Loops Only throughout *(Fig. 2, page 2)*.

Row 2: Turn; slip st in first 5 slip sts, (hdc in next 5 hdc, slip st in next 5 slip sts) across.

Rows 3 and 4: Ch 2, turn; hdc in first 5 sts, (slip st in next 5 sts, hdc in next 5 sts) across.

Row 5: Turn; slip st in first 5 hdc, (hdc in next 5 slip sts, slip st in next 5 hdc) across.

Repeat Rows 2-5 until Dishcloth measures approximately 10" from beginning ch, ending by working a **wrong** side row; do **not** finish off.

Work desired Edging, page 58.

Ch 44.

Row 1 (Right side)**:** 4 Dc in fourth ch from hook, ★ skip next 3 chs, (sc, ch 2, 4 dc) in next ch; repeat from ★ across to last 4 chs, skip next 3 chs, sc in last ch: 50 sts and 10 sps.

Note: Loop a short piece of yarn around any stitch to mark Row 1 as **right** side.

Row 2: Ch 5, turn; 4 dc in fourth ch from hook, ★ skip next ch and next 5 sts, (sc, ch 2, 4 dc) in next ch; repeat from ★ 8 times **more**, skip next ch and next 5 sts, sc in next ch.

Repeat Row 2 until Dishcloth measures approximately 10" from beginning ch, ending by working a **wrong** side row.

Last Row: Ch 3, turn; dc in same st, ch 1, skip next 2 dc, sc in next 2 dc and in next ch-2 sp, ★ ch 1, skip next 3 sts, sc in next 2 dc and in next sp; repeat from ★ across; do **not** finish off.

Work desired Edging, page 58.

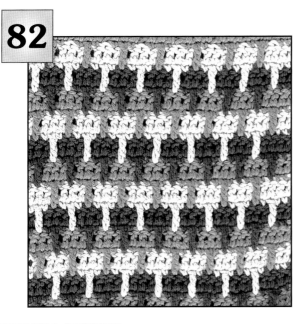

82

STITCH GUIDE
TREBLE CROCHET *(abbreviated tr)*
YO twice, insert hook in st indicated, YO and pull up a loop (4 loops on hook), (YO and draw through 2 loops on hook) 3 times.

With first color, ch 34.

Row 1 (Right side)**:** Sc in second ch from hook and in next ch, ch 1, ★ skip next ch, sc in next 3 chs, ch 1; repeat from ★ across to last 3 chs, skip next ch, sc in last 2 chs: 25 sc and 8 ch-1 sps.

Note: Loop a short piece of yarn around any stitch to mark Row 1 as **right** side.

Row 2: Ch 3 **(counts as first dc, now and throughout)**, turn; dc in next sc, ch 1, ★ skip next ch-1 sp, dc in next 3 sc, ch 1; repeat from ★ across to last ch-1 sp, skip last ch-1 sp, dc in last 2 sc changing to next color in last dc *(Fig. 3a, page 2)*.

Row 3: Ch 1, turn; sc in first 2 dc, working in **front** of previous 2 rows, tr in next skipped ch of beginning ch 2 rows **below**, ★ sc in next dc, ch 1, skip next dc, sc in next dc, working in **front** of previous 2 rows, tr in next skipped ch of beginning ch 2 rows **below**; repeat from ★ across to last 2 dc, sc in last 2 dc: 26 sts and 7 ch-1 sps.

Row 4: Ch 3, turn; dc in next 3 sts, ch 1, ★ skip next ch-1 sp, dc in next 3 sts, ch 1; repeat from ★ across to last ch-1 sp, skip last ch-1 sp, dc in last 4 sts changing to next color in last dc.

Row 5: Ch 1, turn; sc in first 2 dc, ch 1, ★ skip next dc, sc in next dc, working in **front** of previous 2 rows, tr in next skipped dc 2 rows **below**, sc in next dc, ch 1; repeat from ★ across to last 3 dc, skip next dc, sc in last 2 dc: 25 sts and 8 ch-1 sps.

Row 6: Ch 3, turn; dc in next sc, ch 1, ★ skip next ch-1 sp, dc in next 3 sts, ch 1; repeat from ★ across to last ch-1 sp, skip last ch-1 sp, dc in last 2 sc changing to next color in last dc.

Row 7: Ch 1, turn; sc in first 2 dc, working in **front** of previous 2 rows, tr in next skipped dc 2 rows **below**, ★ sc in next dc, ch 1, skip next dc, sc in next dc, working in **front** of previous 2 rows, tr in next skipped dc 2 rows **below**; repeat from ★ across to last 2 dc, sc in last 2 dc: 26 sts and 7 ch-1 sps.

Rows 8-26: Repeat Rows 4-7, 4 times; then repeat Rows 4-6 once **more**; do **not** change colors at end of Row 26 and do **not** finish off.

Work desired Edging, page 58.

83

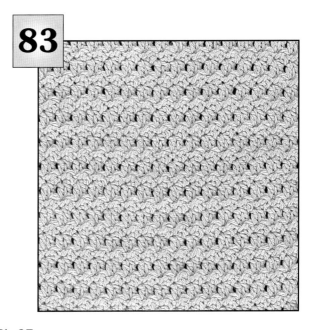

Ch 37.

Row 1 (Right side)**:** Dc in fourth ch from hook **(3 skipped chs count as first dc)** and in each ch across: 35 dc.

Note: Loop a short piece of yarn around any stitch to mark Row 1 as **right** side.

Row 2: Turn; slip st in first dc, (dc in next dc, slip st in next dc) across: 17 dc and 18 slip sts.

Row 3: Ch 3 **(counts as first dc)**, turn; dc in next dc and in each slip st and each dc across: 35 dc.

Repeat Rows 2 and 3 until Dishcloth measures approximately 9" from beginning ch, ending by working Row 3; do **not** finish off.

Work desired Edging, page 58.

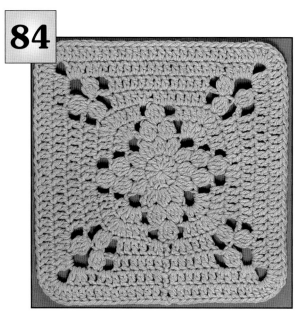

84

STITCH GUIDE

2-DC CLUSTER (uses one st)
★ YO, insert hook in st indicated, YO and pull up a loop, YO and draw through 2 loops on hook; repeat from ★ once **more**, YO and draw through all 3 loops on hook.

3-DC CLUSTER (uses one st or sp)
★ YO, insert hook in st or sp indicated, YO and pull up a loop, YO and draw through 2 loops on hook; repeat from ★ 2 times **more**, YO and draw through all 4 loops on hook.

4-DC CLUSTER (uses one st or sp)
★ YO, insert hook in st or sp indicated, YO and pull up a loop, YO and draw through 2 loops on hook; repeat from ★ 3 times **more**, YO and draw through all 5 loops on hook.

Rnd 1 (Right side)**:** Ch 4, 11 dc in fourth ch from hook; join with slip st to fourth ch of beginning ch-4: 12 sts.

Note: Loop a short piece of yarn around any stitch to mark Rnd 1 as **right** side.

Rnd 2: Ch 3 **(counts as first dc, now and throughout)**, work 2-dc Cluster in same st, (ch 1, work 3-dc Cluster in next dc) twice, ch 5, ★ work 3-dc Cluster in next dc, (ch 1, work 3-dc Cluster in next dc) twice, ch 5; repeat from ★ 2 times **more**; join with slip st to top of first 2-dc Cluster: 12 sps.

Rnd 3: Slip st in first ch-1 sp, ch 3, work 3-dc Cluster in same sp, ch 1, work 4-dc Cluster in next ch-1 sp, ch 2, 5 dc in next ch-5 sp, ch 2, ★ work 4-dc Cluster in next ch-1 sp, ch 1, work 4-dc Cluster in next ch-1 sp, ch 2, 5 dc in next ch-5 sp, ch 2; repeat from ★ 2 times **more**; join with slip st to top of first 3-dc Cluster: 20 dc and 12 sps.

Rnd 4: Slip st in first ch-1 sp, ch 3, work 3-dc Cluster in same sp, ch 2, dc in next ch-2 sp and in next 2 dc, 5 dc in next dc, dc in next 2 dc and in next ch-2 sp, ch 2, ★ work 4-dc Cluster in next ch-1 sp, ch 2, dc in next ch-2 sp and in next 2 dc, 5 dc in next dc, dc in next 2 dc and in next ch-2 sp, ch 2; repeat from ★ 2 times **more**; join with slip st to top of first 3-dc Cluster: 48 sts and 8 ch-2 sps.

Rnd 5: Ch 3, 2 dc in next ch-2 sp, dc in next 4 dc, ch 3, skip next dc, work 4-dc Cluster in next dc, ch 3, skip next dc, dc in next 4 dc, 2 dc in next ch-2 sp, ★ dc in next 4-dc Cluster, 2 dc in next ch-2 sp, dc in next 4 dc, ch 3, skip next dc, work 4-dc Cluster in next dc, ch 3, skip next dc, dc in next 4 dc, 2 dc in next ch-2 sp; repeat from ★ 2 times **more**; join with slip st to first dc: 52 dc and 8 ch-3 sps.

Rnd 6: Ch 3, dc in next 6 dc, ch 2, skip next 2 chs, work 4-dc Cluster in next ch, ch 5, skip next 4-dc Cluster, work 4-dc Cluster in next ch, ch 2, ★ dc in next 13 dc, ch 2, skip next 2 chs, work 4-dc Cluster in next ch, ch 5, skip next 4-dc Cluster, work 4-dc Cluster in next ch, ch 2; repeat from ★ 2 times **more**, dc in last 6 dc; join with slip st to first dc: 52 dc and 12 sps.

Rnd 7: Ch 3, dc in next 6 dc, 2 dc in next ch-2 sp, dc in next 4-dc Cluster, (3 dc, ch 3, 3 dc) in next ch-5 sp, dc in next 4-dc Cluster, 2 dc in next ch-2 sp, ★ dc in next 13 dc, 2 dc in next ch-2 sp, dc in next 4-dc Cluster, (3 dc, ch 3, 3 dc) in next ch-5 sp, dc in next 4-dc Cluster, 2 dc in next ch-2 sp; repeat from ★ 2 times **more**, dc in last 6 dc; join with slip st to first dc: 100 dc and 4 ch-3 sps.

Rnd 8: Ch 3, (dc in each dc across to next ch-3 sp, 5 dc in ch-3 sp) 3 times, dc in last 12 dc; join with slip st to first dc, do **not** finish off.

Work desired Edging, page 58.

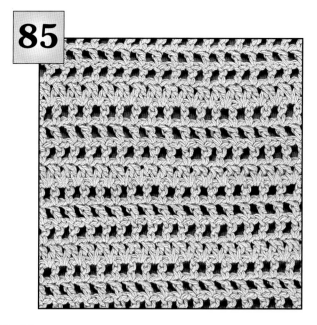

85

Ch 43.

Row 1 (Right side)**:** Dc in fourth ch from hook **(3 skipped chs count as first dc)** and in each ch across: 41 dc.

Note: Loop a short piece of yarn around any stitch to mark Row 1 as **right** side.

Row 2: Ch 4 **(counts as first dc plus ch 1, now and throughout)**, turn; skip next dc, dc in next dc, ★ ch 1, skip next dc, dc in next dc; repeat from ★ across: 21 dc and 20 ch-1 sps.

Rows 3 and 4: Ch 4, turn; dc in next dc, (ch 1, dc in next dc) across.

Row 5: Ch 4, turn; (YO, insert hook in **next** ch-1 sp, YO and pull up a loop, YO and draw through 2 loops on hook) twice, YO and draw through all 3 loops on hook, ch 1, ★ YO, insert hook in same ch-1 sp, YO and pull up a loop, YO and draw through 2 loops on hook, YO, insert hook in next ch-1 sp, YO and pull up a loop, YO and draw through 2 loops on hook, YO and draw through all 3 loops on hook, ch 1; repeat from ★ across to last dc, dc in last dc.

Row 6: Ch 4, turn; skip first ch, dc in next st, ★ ch 1, skip next ch, dc in next st; repeat from ★ across.

Repeat Rows 3-6 until Dishcloth measures approximately 10" from beginning ch, ending by working Row 4.

Last Row: Ch 3, turn; dc in each ch-1 sp and in each dc across; do **not** finish off.

Work desired Edging, page 58.

Design by Linda Luder.

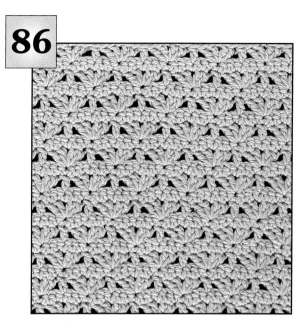

86

STITCH GUIDE
SHELL
(2 Dc, ch 1, 2 dc) in st indicated.

___

Ch 45.

Row 1 (Right side)**:** Work Shell in sixth ch from hook, skip next 2 chs, dc in next ch, ★ skip next 2 chs, work Shell in next ch, skip next 2 chs, dc in next ch; repeat from ★ across: 7 Shells.

Note: Loop a short piece of yarn around any stitch to mark Row 1 as **right** side.

Row 2: Ch 1, turn; sc in first 3 dc and in next ch-1 sp, (sc in next 5 dc and in next ch-1 sp) 6 times, sc in next 2 dc and in next ch: 43 sc.

Row 3: Ch 3 **(counts as first dc, now and throughout)**, turn; 2 dc in same st, skip next 2 sc, dc in next sc, ★ skip next 2 sc, work Shell in next sc, skip next 2 sc, dc in next sc; repeat from ★ across to last 3 sc, skip next 2 sc, 3 dc in last sc: 6 Shells.

Row 4: Ch 1, turn; sc in first 6 dc and in next ch-1 sp, (sc in next 5 dc and in next ch-1 sp) 5 times, sc in last 6 dc: 43 sc.

Row 5: Ch 3, turn; ★ skip next 2 sc, work Shell in next sc, skip next 2 sc, dc in next sc; repeat from ★ across: 7 Shells.

Row 6: Ch 1, turn; sc in first 3 dc and in next ch-1 sp, (sc in next 5 dc and in next ch-1 sp) across to last 3 dc, sc in last 3 dc: 43 sc.

Rows 7-25: Repeat Rows 3-6, 4 times, then repeat Rows 3-5 once **more**; do **not** finish off.

Work desired Edging, page 58.

Design by Linda Luder.

50

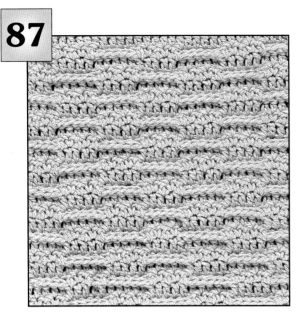

Ch 37.

Row 1 (Right side)**:** Dc in fourth ch from hook **(3 skipped chs count as first dc)** and in each ch across: 35 dc.

Note: Loop a short piece of yarn around any stitch to mark Row 1 as **right** side.

Row 2: Ch 1, turn; sc from **front** to **back** around each post of first 5 dc *(Fig. 4, page 2)*, ★ dc in next dc, (sc in next dc, dc in next dc) twice, sc from **front** to **back** around each post of next 5 dc; repeat from ★ 2 times **more**.

Row 3: Ch 3 **(counts as first dc, now and throughout)**, turn; dc in next sc and in each st across.

Row 4: Ch 1, turn; sc in first 2 dc, dc in next dc, sc in next dc, dc in next dc, sc from **front** to **back** around each post of next 5 dc, ★ dc in next dc, (sc in next dc, dc in next dc) twice, sc from **front** to **back** around each post of next 5 dc; repeat from ★ once **more**, dc in next dc, sc in next dc, dc in next dc, sc in last 2 dc.

Row 5: Ch 3, turn; dc in next sc and in each st across.

Repeat Rows 2-5 until Dishcloth measures approximately 9¹/₂" from beginning ch, ending by working a **right** side row; do **not** finish off.

Work desired Edging, page 58.

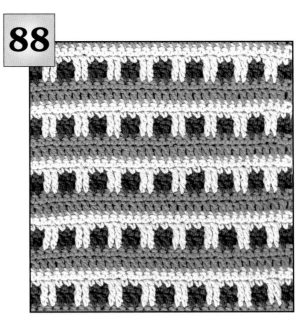

STITCH GUIDE
TREBLE CROCHET *(abbreviated tr)*
YO twice, insert hook in sc indicated, YO and pull up a loop (4 loops on hook), (YO and draw through 2 loops on hook) 3 times.

With first color, ch 40.

Row 1 (Right side)**:** Dc in fourth ch from hook **(3 skipped chs count as first dc)** and in each ch across: 38 dc.

Note: Loop a short piece of yarn around any stitch to mark Row 1 as **right** side.

Row 2: Ch 1, turn; sc in each dc across changing to next color in last sc *(Fig. 3a, page 2)*.

Row 3: Ch 3 **(counts as first dc, now and throughout)**, turn; dc in next sc, ★ ch 2, skip next 2 sc, dc in next 2 sc; repeat from ★ across: 20 dc and 9 ch-2 sps.

Row 4: Ch 1, turn; sc in first 2 dc, ★ ch 2, skip next ch-2 sp, sc in next 2 dc; repeat from ★ across changing to next color in last sc.

Row 5: Ch 1, turn; sc in first 2 sc, ★ working in **front** of previous 2 rows, tr in 2 skipped sc 2 rows **below**, sc in next 2 sc; repeat from ★ across: 38 sts.

Row 6: Ch 1, turn; sc in each st across changing to next color in last sc.

Row 7: Ch 3, turn; dc in next sc and in each sc across.

Row 8: Ch 1, turn; sc in each dc across changing to next color in last sc.

Repeat Rows 3-8 until Dishcloth measures approximately 9¹/₂" from beginning ch, ending by working Row 8; do **not** change colors at end of last row and do **not** finish off.

Work desired Edging, page 58.

51

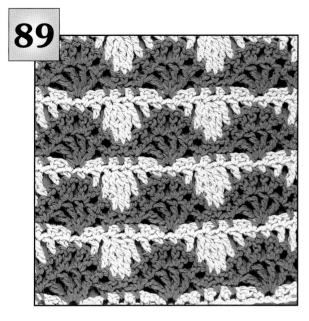

89

STITCH GUIDE

TREBLE CROCHET *(abbreviated tr)*
YO twice, insert hook in st or sp indicated, YO and pull up a loop (4 loops on hook), (YO and draw through 2 loops on hook) 3 times.

DOUBLE TREBLE CROCHET *(abbreviated dtr)*
YO 3 times, insert hook in st indicated, YO and pull up a loop (5 loops on hook), (YO and draw through 2 loops on hook) 4 times.

DECREASE (uses next 2 sts)
★ YO 3 times, insert hook **next** st, YO and pull up a loop, (YO and draw through 2 loops on hook) 3 times; repeat from ★ once **more**, YO and draw through all 3 loops on hook.

DOUBLE DECREASE (uses next 3 sts)
★ YO 3 times, insert hook **next** st, YO and pull up a loop, (YO and draw through 2 loops on hook) 3 times; repeat from ★ 2 times **more**, YO and draw through all 4 loops on hook.

With first color, ch 38.

Row 1 (Wrong side)**:** Sc in second ch from hook and in next ch, ch 1, ★ skip next ch, sc in next ch, ch 1; repeat from ★ across to last 3 chs, skip next ch, sc in last 2 chs changing to next color in last sc *(Fig. 3a, page 2)*: 20 sc and 17 ch-1 sps.

Note: Loop a short piece of yarn around **back** of any stitch on Row 1 to mark **right** side.

Row 2: Ch 1, turn; sc in first sc, ch 1, sc in next ch-1 sp, ch 1, skip next ch-1 sp, (tr, ch 1) 4 times in next ch-1 sp, skip next ch-1 sp, ★ (sc in next ch-1 sp, ch 1) 3 times, skip next ch-1 sp, (tr, ch 1) 4 times in next ch-1 sp, skip next ch-1 sp; repeat from ★ once **more**, sc in next ch-1 sp, ch 1, skip next sc, sc in last sc: 22 sts and 21 ch-1 sps.

Row 3: Ch 1, turn; sc in first sc, ★ dc in next sc, ch 1, dc in next tr, ch 1, (dc, ch 1) twice in next 2 tr, dc in next tr, ch 1, dc in next sc, sc in next sc; repeat from ★ 2 times **more** changing to next color in last sc: 28 sts and 21 ch-1 sps.

Row 4: Ch 4, turn; skip first sc, dtr in next dc, tr in next dc, ch 1, dc in next dc, ch 1, (sc in next dc, ch 1) twice, dc in next dc, ch 1, tr in next dc, skip next ch-1 sp, ★ double decrease, tr in next dc, ch 1, dc in next dc, ch 1, (sc in next dc, ch 1) twice, dc in next dc, ch 1, tr in next dc, skip next ch-1 sp; repeat from ★ once **more**, decrease: 23 sts and 15 ch-1 sps.

Row 5: Ch 1, turn; sc in first 2 sts, (ch 1, skip next ch-1 sp, sc in next st) 5 times, ★ ch 1, skip next st, sc in next st, (ch 1, skip next ch-1 sp, sc in next st) 5 times; repeat from ★ once **more**, skip next dtr, sc in next ch changing to next color: 20 sc and 17 ch-1 sps.

Repeat Rows 2-5 until Dishcloth measures approximately 9" from beginning ch, ending by working Row 5; do **not** change colors at end of last row and do **not** finish off.

Work desired Edging, page 58.

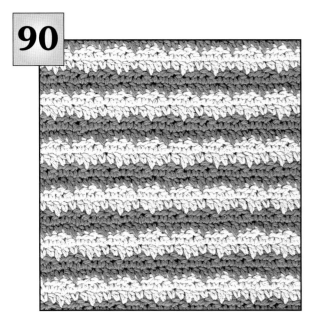

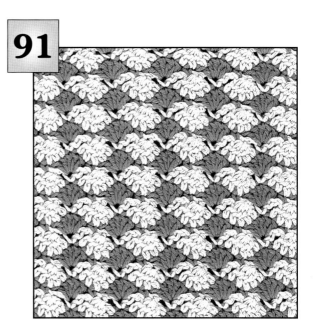

With first color, ch 38.

Row 1 (Right side)**:** Sc in second ch from hook, ★ hdc in next ch, dc in next ch, hdc in next ch, sc in next ch; repeat from ★ across: 37 sts.

Note #1: Loop a short piece of yarn around any stitch to mark Row 1 as **right** side.

Note #2: Do **not** cut yarn unless otherwise instructed. Carry unused yarn **loosely** along end of rows.

Row 2: Ch 1, turn; sc in first sc, ★ hdc in next hdc, dc in next dc, hdc in next hdc, sc in next sc; repeat from ★ across changing to next color in last sc *(Fig. 3a, page 2)*.

Row 3: Ch 3 **(counts as first dc, now and throughout)**, turn; ★ hdc in next hdc, sc in next dc, hdc in next hdc, dc in next sc; repeat from ★ across.

Row 4: Ch 3, turn; ★ hdc in next hdc, sc in next sc, hdc in next hdc, dc in next dc; repeat from ★ across changing to next color in last dc.

Row 5: Ch 1, turn; sc in first dc, ★ hdc in next hdc, dc in next sc, hdc in next hdc, sc in next dc; repeat from ★ across.

Repeat Rows 2-5 until Dishcloth measures approximately 9" from beginning ch, ending by working Row 2, do **not** change colors at end of last row, cut previous color; do **not** finish off.

Work desired Edging, page 58.

STITCH GUIDE
CLUSTER (uses next 5 sts)
★ YO, insert hook in **next** st, YO and pull up a loop, YO and draw through 2 loops on hook; repeat from ★ 4 times **more**, YO and draw through all 6 loops on hook.

With first color, ch 46.

Row 1 (Right side)**:** 2 Dc in fourth ch from hook **(3 skipped chs count as first dc)**, skip next 2 chs, sc in next ch, ★ skip next 2 chs, 5 dc in next ch, skip next 2 chs, sc in next ch; repeat from ★ across to last 3 chs, skip next 2 chs, 3 dc in last ch changing to next color in last dc *(Fig. 3a, page 2)*: 43 sts.

Note: Loop a short piece of yarn around any stitch to mark Row 1 as **right** side.

Row 2: Ch 1, turn; sc in first dc, ★ ch 2, work Cluster, ch 2, sc in next dc; repeat from ★ across changing to next color in last sc: 7 Clusters and 14 ch-2 sps.

Row 3: Ch 3 **(counts as first dc)**, turn; 2 dc in same st, skip next ch-2 sp, sc in next Cluster, ★ skip next ch-2 sp, 5 dc in next sc, skip next ch-2 sp, sc in next Cluster; repeat from ★ across to last ch-2 sp, skip last ch-2 sp, 3 dc in last sc changing to next color in last dc: 43 sts.

Repeat Rows 2 and 3 until Dishcloth measures approximately 10" from beginning ch, ending by working Row 3; do **not** change colors at end of last row and do **not** finish off.

Work desired Edging, page 58.

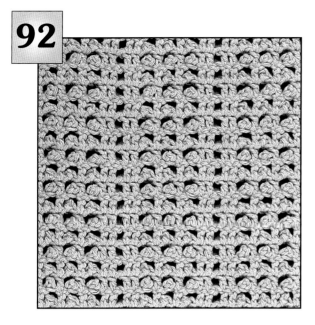

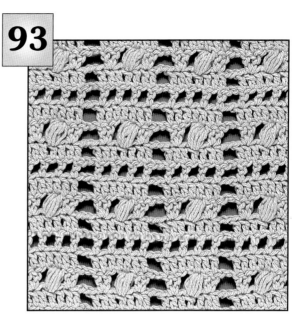

STITCH GUIDE
PICOT
Ch 3, slip st in third ch from hook.

Ch 33.

Row 1 (Right side)**:** Dc in fourth ch from hook **(3 skipped chs count as first dc)** and in next ch, work Picot, ch 1, (skip next ch, dc in next ch, work Picot, ch 1) twice, ★ skip next ch, dc in next 2 chs, ch 1, skip next ch, dc in next 2 chs, work Picot, ch 1, (skip next ch, dc in next ch, work Picot, ch 1) twice; repeat from ★ once **more**, skip next ch, dc in last 3 chs: 20 dc.

Note: Loop a short piece of yarn around any stitch to mark Row 1 as **right** side.

Row 2: Ch 3 **(counts as first dc, now and throughout)**, turn; dc in next 2 dc, work Picot, ch 1, skip next Picot, dc in next dc, work Picot, ch 1) twice, ★ skip next Picot, dc in next 2 dc, ch 1, dc in next 2 dc, work Picot, ch 1, (skip next Picot, dc in next dc, work Picot, ch 1) twice; repeat from ★ once **more**, skip next Picot, dc in last 3 dc.

Repeat Row 2 until Dishcloth measures approximately 9½" from beginning ch.

Last Row: Ch 3, turn; dc in next 2 dc, ch 1, (skip next Picot, dc in next dc, ch 1) twice, ★ skip next Picot, dc in next 2 dc, ch 1, dc in next 2 dc, ch 1, (skip next Picot, dc in next dc, ch 1) twice; repeat from ★ once **more**, skip next Picot, dc in last 3 dc; do **not** finish off.

Work desired Edging, page 58.

STITCH GUIDE
PUFF ST (uses one dc)
★ YO, insert hook in dc indicated, YO and pull up a loop; repeat from ★ 4 times **more**, YO and draw through all 11 loops on hook.

Ch 44.

Row 1 (Right side)**:** Dc in fourth ch from hook **(3 skipped chs count as first dc)**, ch 2, ★ skip next 2 chs, dc in next 7 chs, ch 2; repeat from ★ across to last 4 chs, skip next 2 chs, dc in last 2 chs: 32 dc and 5 ch-2 sps.

Note: Loop a short piece of yarn around any stitch to mark Row 1 as **right** side.

Row 2: Ch 3 **(counts as first dc now and throughout)**, turn; dc in next dc, ch 2, ★ skip next ch-2 sp and next dc, 2 dc in next dc, ch 1, skip next dc, work Puff St in next dc, ch 1, skip next dc, 2 dc in next dc, ch 2; repeat from ★ across to last ch-2 sp, skip last ch-2 sp, dc in last 2 dc: 24 sts and 13 sps.

Row 3: Ch 3, turn; dc in next dc, ch 2, ★ skip next ch-2 sp, dc in each st and in each ch across to next ch-2 sp, ch 2; repeat from ★ across to last ch-2 sp, skip last ch-2 sp, dc in last 2 dc: 32 dc and 5 ch-2 sps.

Row 4: Ch 3, turn; dc in next dc, ch 2, ★ dc in next dc, (ch 1, skip next dc, dc in next dc) 3 times, ch 2; repeat from ★ across to last 2 dc, dc in last 2 dc: 20 dc and 17 sps.

Row 5: Ch 3, turn; dc in next dc, ch 2, ★ dc in next dc, (dc in next ch and in next dc) 3 times, ch 2; repeat from ★ across to last 2 dc, dc in last 2 dc: 32 dc and 5 ch-2 sps.

Repeat Rows 2-5 until Dishcloth measures approximately 10½" from beginning ch, ending by working Row 3; do **not** finish off.

Work desired Edging, page 58.

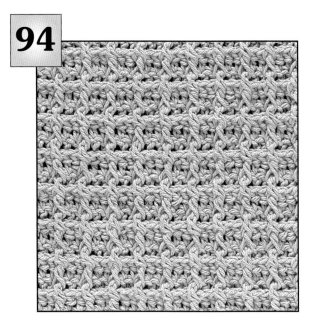

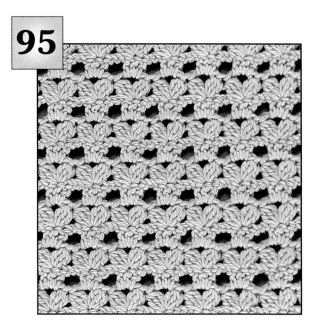

STITCH GUIDE
FRONT POST DOUBLE CROCHET
(abbreviated FPdc)
YO, insert hook from **front** to **back** around post of st indicated *(Fig. 4, page 2)*, YO and pull up a loop (3 loops on hook), (YO and draw through 2 loops on hook) twice.

BACK POST DOUBLE CROCHET
(abbreviated BPdc)
YO, insert hook from **back** to **front** around post of st indicated *(Fig. 4, page 2)*, YO and pull up a loop (3 loops on hook), (YO and draw through 2 loops on hook) twice.

———————————————

Ch 39.

Row 1 (Right side)**:** Dc in fourth ch from hook **(3 skipped chs count as first dc)** and in each ch across: 37 dc.

Note: Loop a short piece of yarn around any stitch to mark Row 1 as **right** side.

Row 2: Ch 3 **(counts as first dc, now and throughout)**, turn; work FPdc around each of next 2 dc, (work BPdc around next dc, work FPdc around each of next 2 dc) across to last dc, dc in last dc.

Row 3: Ch 3, turn; (dc in next 2 FPdc, work FPdc around next BPdc) across to last 3 sts, dc in last 3 sts.

Row 4: Ch 3, turn; work FPdc around each of next 2 dc, (work BPdc around next FPdc, work FPdc around each of next 2 dc) across to last dc, dc in last dc.

Repeat Rows 3 and 4 until Dishcloth measures approximately 9¹/₂" from beginning ch, ending by working Row 3, do **not** finish off.

Work desired Edging, page 58.

STITCH GUIDE
CLUSTER (uses one dc)
★ YO, insert hook in dc indicated, YO and pull up a loop, YO and draw through 2 loops on hook; repeat from ★ 2 times **more**, YO and draw through all 4 loops on hook.

———————————————

Ch 39.

Row 1: Dc in fourth ch from hook **(3 skipped chs count as first dc)** and in next 2 chs, ch 2, ★ skip next ch, dc in next 3 chs, ch 2; repeat from ★ across to last 5 chs, skip next ch, dc in last 4 chs: 29 dc and 8 ch-2 sps.

Row 2 (Right side)**:** Ch 3 **(counts as first dc, now and throughout)**, turn; skip next dc, work (Cluster, ch 3, Cluster) in next dc, ★ skip next 2 dc, work (Cluster, ch 3, Cluster) in next dc; repeat from ★ across to last 2 dc, skip next dc, dc in last dc: 18 Clusters and 9 ch-3 sps.

Note: Loop a short piece of yarn around any stitch to mark Row 2 as **right** side.

Row 3: Ch 3, turn; 3 dc in next ch-3 sp, (ch 2, 3 dc in next ch-3 sp) across to last dc, dc in last dc: 29 dc and 8 ch-2 sps.

Row 4: Ch 3, turn; skip next dc, work (Cluster, ch 3, Cluster) in next dc, ★ skip next 2 dc, work (Cluster, ch 3, Cluster) in next dc; repeat from ★ across to last 2 dc, skip next dc, dc in last dc: 18 Clusters and 9 ch-3 sps.

Repeat Rows 3 and 4 until Dishcloth measures approximately 10¹/₂" from beginning ch, ending by working Row 3; do **not** finish off.

Work desired Edging, page 58.

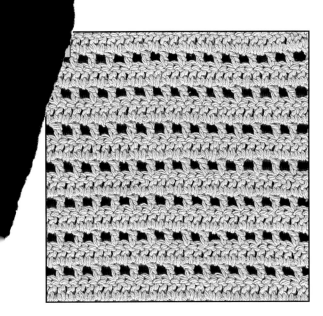

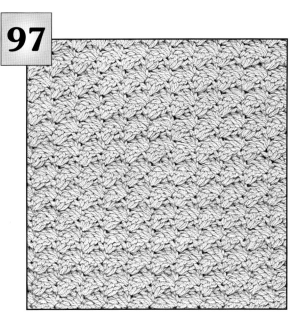

Ch 37.

Row 1 (Wrong side): Dc in fourth ch from hook **(3 skipped chs count as first dc)** and in each ch across: 35 dc.

Note: Loop a short piece of yarn around **back** of any stitch on Row 1 to mark **right** side.

Row 2: Ch 4 **(counts as first dc plus ch 1)**, turn; skip next dc, dc in next dc, ★ ch 1, skip next dc, dc in next dc; repeat from ★ across: 18 dc and 17 ch-1 sps.

Row 3: Ch 3 **(counts as first dc)**, turn; dc in next ch-1 sp and in each dc and each ch-1 sp across: 35 dc.

Repeat Rows 2 and 3 until Dishcloth measures approximately 9" from beginning ch, ending by working Row 3; do **not** finish off.

Work desired Edging, page 58.

Design by Darla Sims.

Ch 38.

Row 1 (Right side): (Sc, 2 dc) in second ch from hook, ★ skip next 2 chs, (sc, 2 dc) in next ch; repeat from ★ across to last 3 chs, skip next 2 chs, sc in last ch: 37 sts.

Note: Loop a short piece of yarn around any stitch to mark Row 1 as **right** side.

Row 2: Ch 1, turn; (sc, 2 dc) in first sc, ★ skip next 2 dc, (sc, 2 dc) in next sc; repeat from ★ across to last 3 sts, skip next 2 dc, sc in last sc.

Repeat Row 2 until Dishcloth measures approximately 9½" from beginning ch, ending by working a **wrong** side row; do **not** finish off.

Work desired Edging, page 58.

Design by Darla Sims.

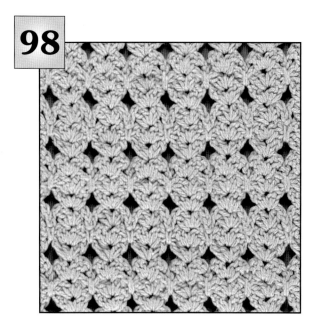

98

Ch 43.

Row 1 (Right side)**:** 2 Dc in fifth ch from hook, ch 1, 2 dc in next ch, ★ skip next 3 chs, 2 dc in next ch, ch 1, 2 dc in next ch; repeat from ★ across to last 2 chs, skip next ch, dc in last ch: 34 sts and 8 ch-1 sps.

Note: Loop a short piece of yarn around any stitch to mark Row 1 as **right** side.

Row 2: Ch 3, turn; (2 dc, ch 1, 2 dc) in each ch-1 sp across to last 2 dc, skip last 2 dc, dc in next ch.

Row 3: Ch 3, turn; (2 dc, ch 1, 2 dc) in next ch-1 sp, ★ ch 2, skip next 2 dc, sc **tightly** around sp of last 2 rows *(Fig. 13)*, ch 2, (2 dc, ch 1, 2 dc) in next ch-1 sp; repeat from ★ across to last 2 dc, skip last 2 dc, dc in next ch: 41 sts and 22 sps.

Fig. 13

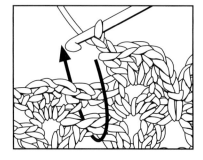

Row 4: Ch 3, turn; (2 dc, ch 1, 2 dc) in next ch-1 sp, ★ skip next 2 ch-2 sps, (2 dc, ch 1, 2 dc) in next ch-1 sp; repeat from ★ across to last 2 dc, skip last 2 dc, dc in next ch: 34 sts and 8 ch-1 sps.

Row 5: Ch 3, turn; (2 dc, ch 1, 2 dc) in each ch-1 sp across to last 2 dc, skip last 2 dc, dc in next ch.

Repeat Rows 3-5 until Dishcloth measures approximately 10" from beginning ch, ending by working Row 4 or Row 5; do **not** finish off.

Work desired Edging, page 58.

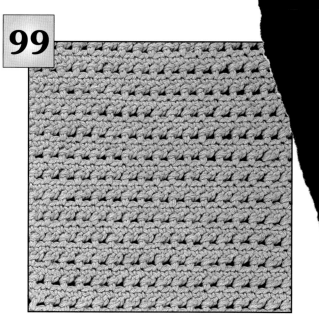

99

Ch 37.

Row 1 (Right side)**:** Sc in second ch from hook and in each ch across: 36 sc.

Note: Loop a short piece of yarn around any stitch to mark Row 1 as **right** side.

Row 2: Ch 2, turn; skip first sc, hdc in next sc, hdc from **front** to **back** around post of hdc just made *(Fig. 4, page 2)*, ★ skip next sc, hdc in next sc, hdc from **front** to **back** around post of hdc just made; repeat from ★ across to last 2 sc, skip next sc, hdc in last sc.

Row 3: Ch 1, turn; working in horizontal ridge of each hdc *(Fig. 14)*, sc in each hdc across, sc in next ch.

Fig. 14

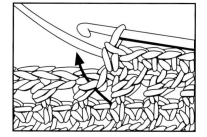

Repeat Rows 2 and 3 until Dishcloth measures approximately 9" from beginning ch, ending by working Row 3; do **not** finish off.

Work desired Edging, page 58.